KNIT Ponchos, Wraps & Scarves

JANE DAVIS

©2005 by Jane Davis

Published by

kp books
An Imprint of F+W Publications

700 East State Street • Iola, WI 54990-0001
715-445-2214 • 888-457-2873

Library of Congress Catalog Number: 2004097731
ISBN: 0-87349-965-4

Edited by Maria L. Turner
Designed by Emily Adler

Printed in the United States of America

Acknowledgments

This book has been a joy to make. The only difficult part was finally having to stop designing to get it all to my editor on time. So, thanks once again to my fabulous editor, Maria Turner, for your editing expertise and deadlines that brought it all together. It is always a joy to work with you.

Many thanks to all the people at KP Books, who helped so much in the process of getting this book to print, beginning with Julie Stephani in acquisitions to Emily Adler in the art department who set up the wonderful page layout and design and Marilyn McGrane for the cover design.

Thank you to Lois Varga, owner of Anacapa Fine Yarns in Ventura, Calif., (www.anacapafineyarns.com) for the use of your manikins and your store for some of the photography, and for including your white scarf design in this book. But thank you more for opening such a wonderful yarn shop in Ventura, and for your warm friendly smile every time I enter the store. It is so nice to have you as a friend.

Finally, a very special thank you to all the yarn companies who have provided yarn for projects in this book! Who knew that making simple strips of knitting could be such an adventure? It would not have been possible without the creativity and experimentation sprouting forth from all these fine yarn companies. Your yarn is delectable!

- Artful Yarns
- Baabajoe's
- Berroco
- Blue Sky Alpacas
- Brown Sheep
- Cascade Yarns
- Classic Elite Yarns
- Crystal Palace Yarns
- Dale of Norway
- Filatura Di Crosa
- Harrisville Designs
- Ironstone Yarns
- Jaeger
- Knit One Crochet Too
- Lion Brand Yarn
- Lorna's Laces
- Patons
- Plymouth
- Rowan
- S. Charles Callezione
- Tahki Stacy Charles
- Trendsetter Yarns

Table of Contents

Introduction

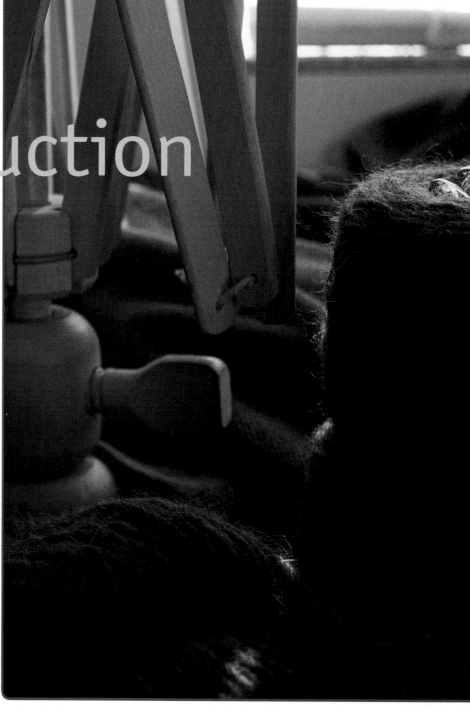

Scarves are great fun to knit. After all, you don't have to worry about the size or the fit. You can just pick a yarn and knit until you want to stop. They are beautiful accessories, and they make great gifts. And with all the yarns available today, you don't have to know a lot about knitting to make something spectacular; just get a gorgeous yarn, cast on and work in easy garter or stockinette stitch until the yarn runs out. Shawls, wraps and ponchos can be just as easy as scarves, though they do take more time and yarn.

Scarves and wraps are also great projects to try out new techniques or make mini masterpieces. You don't have to be the kind of person who wears them to enjoy them either. They can be displayed at home on a hook or quilt rack, or over a chair to add ambience to a room. And there is so much room for detail, from I-cord experimentation to intricate fringe detailing and beadwork to all levels of embroidery.

Collected here are more than 40 designs to whet your appetite for knitting scarves. They range from quick and easy beginner garter stitch projects to elegant beaded scarves, a large lacework shawl and several trendy ponchos. A variety of novelty yarns are presented and discussed, from the thin railroad yarn or sequins spaced on thread to the fluffy, nontraditional eyelash yarn that will probably be the hallmark of these current years in knitting. The classics are not neglected, though they are often updated by using beautiful colors in hand-dyed hues.

The last section focuses on fringes and edgings, and even with more than 10 projects in that section, it really only touches on the possibilities.

So take a look, then start to plan your next scarf. Will it be quick and easy with novelty yarn, or large and detailed, to have on display enhancing your home décor?

Whatever you choose, I hope you enjoy making your next scarf, wrap or poncho.

Basics

Although it's easy to make a scarf with simple knit or knit and purl stitches, there's a lot more for you to explore. Here you will find interesting facts and useful information about ponchos, scarves and wraps, and basic knitting techniques for working with yarn. A fun reference is the list of names of scarves and scarf-like accessories. The list of types of novelty yarns helps make sense of all the new yarns on the market. If ponchos are your interest, you'll want to read the basics on how to make several types of ponchos, and how to turn shawls, wraps and scarves into ponchos. Finally, the illustrated knitting how-to section is a quick refresher on techniques used for projects in this book.

What is a Scarf or Shawl?

And what are all those other names that are used for similar shapes that you wrap around your neck and shoulders? Here is a vocabulary list of scarf and shawl accessories, from a minimal bolo to a long cloak. Some are old terms that aren't used much today, if at all, and some have interesting origins that are fun to discover.

Ascot: A small scarf, originally worn by men, that is wrapped around the neck and knotted so the wide ends overlap and are sometimes secured with a decorative pin. The name comes from Ascot, England, where the famous horse race is held every year and where the scarf style was popularized.

Bandana: A large handkerchief, usually with a solid background of red or blue, with simple light-colored designs.

Bolo tie: A long, thin cord hung around the neck and secured with a decorative ornament.

Cape: A garment, fastened at the neck, that has no sleeves and drapes over your shoulders in either a short or long length.

Capelet: A short version of a cape that just covers the shoulders.

Cloak: Similar to a cape, though usually thought of as longer, to the ankles.

Comforter: A long, narrow scarf, commonly knitted.

Cravat: A scarf often trimmed with lace and worn as a necktie. Named for the 17th century Croatian mercenaries working for France who wore linen scarves.

Fichu: A medium-sized triangular scarf worn by women, which is usually made of thin, light fabric draped over the shoulders and tied in the front.

Handkerchief: A small, usually square piece of cloth, sometimes edged in lace or made of printed or embroidered fabric, that is used as a decorative accessory in the upper jacket pocket of a man's suit, or functionally used to wipe the eyes or nose.

Mantilla: A lightweight scarf, usually black lace, worn over the head and shoulders, commonly by Spanish and Latin American women.

Muffler: A scarf or veil worn about the neck or as a veil to conceal.

Neckerchief: A square of fabric folded diagonally and tied around the neck, commonly worn by sailors as a part of their uniform.

Poncho: Originally from South America, a blanket or cloak with a hole in the middle to put the head through. It is worn over clothing like a jacket.

Ruff: A stiffened wheel of lace worn close around the neck by men and women during the 16th and 17th centuries, as in the famous paintings of Mary Queen of Scots.

Serape: Also spelled "sarape," a wool blanket, usually woven in bright colors, worn as a poncho by Latin American men.

Scarf: A piece of fabric, which can vary in width and length, worn around the neck, head, waist, hips and/or shoulders for warmth or fashion.

Shawl: A large, folded square or large triangle-shaped piece of fabric worn by women around the head, neck and shoulders.

Stole: A long, wide rectangular scarf, worn by women around the neck and shoulders.

Tie or necktie: A narrow piece of fabric tied at the neck into a knot with the ends hanging loose or tied into a bow (bow tie).

Wrap: A garment, such as a large scarf, that is wrapped around the shoulders, as though it were a shawl.

A GUIDE TO SCARF LENGTHS

Here is my personal rule of thumb for scarf lengths, not including fringe.

Ascot length (32" to 40"): Just enough to go around the back of your neck with both ends hanging in front.

Traditional scarf (45" to 50"): Enough to wrap once around your neck with one end in front and the other over your shoulder hanging in back.

Long scarf (60" to 80"): Enough to wrap twice around your neck with the ends both in the front; one in back, one in front; or both in back.

Anatomy of a Poncho

Ponchos are very versatile garments that are easy to make from simple geometric shapes, such as rectangles, triangles or squares. You can make them in one piece from end to end, or knit them in two pieces and sew them together at the shoulders. You can knit them from the bottom to the top, from the top down or from side to side. Your finished poncho can be worn symmetrically with a point at the bottom center front and back or with the points off-center, depending on the type of poncho created.

Illustrated here are four ways of making a poncho.

Figures 1-1A, B and C show how to take two rectangles and sew them together so that you use both the sides and the ends of the rectangles to create the neck opening. This style can be worn with the point at the center or at the side of your body.

12" to 24" wide by 28" to 42" long

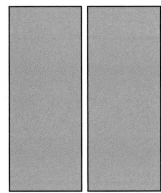

Figure 1-1A

Figures 1-2A, B and C show how to take a single rectangle, fold it in half and then seam only a portion of the sides together to make the neck opening. This creates an asymmetrical poncho.

Figure 1-2A

Figures 1-3A and B show a serape design, which is just a rectangle with a hole in the middle for your head.

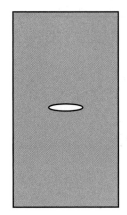

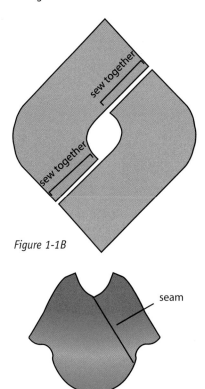

sew together

sew together

Figure 1-1B

seam

Figure 1-1C

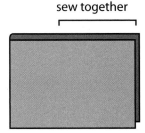

sew together

Figure 1-2B

seam

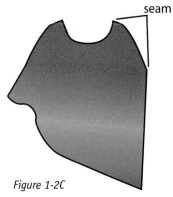

Figure 1-2C

Figure 1-3A

Figure 1-3B

Finally, Figures 1-4A and B show how the last shape is created when you take two triangles and sew them together, leaving an opening for your head. It's the classic poncho design.

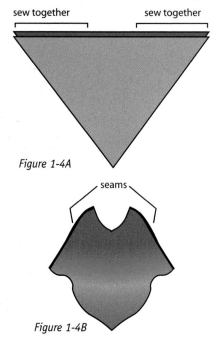

Figure 1-4A

Figure 1-4B

There are other ways to make ponchos too, including making circles, tubes and gores. Any shapes you can craft into a tapered covering with an opening for your head can become a beautiful poncho made of beautiful yarn.

Your main concerns when making a poncho are the size of the neck opening and the length of the sides and front from the neckline. Generally, the neckline opening needs to be between 22" circumference for a tight-fitting neckline to 36" circumference for a low neckline opening.

The length of your poncho is up to you, but you will probably want it to go at least to your elbows, which would be 12" at the very least, or maybe all the way to your wrists, which is about 24". If you are going to add fringe, take that added length into consideration when planning your design.

When making a poncho from the patterns in this book, always try it on, or hold it up to you as you are working so you see if it is the right size for you. It's easy to make it longer or shorter to fit your own size.

MAKING SCARVES INTO PONCHOS

Many of the projects in this book are easy to transform from shawls and wraps into ponchos.

For triangle shawls, you can simply make two and sew them together, leaving an opening in the middle for your head.

Any basic rectangle can be made in duplicate and then sewn together, as the Easy Evening Poncho was constructed on page 52.

Really, just about any scarf can be made into a poncho by making it wide and casting off some of the center stitches. Then knitting the sides for a few rows, casting on the center stitches again and knitting across all the stitches until both sides are the same length. This creates a serape-style poncho with a straight front and back edge that tapers down at the sides, as in the Bold Stripes Serape Style Poncho on page 44.

The Easy Evening Poncho, shown here and detailed on pages 52 and 53, began as two basic rectangles and was sewn together to create a poncho.

The Bold Stripes Serape-Style Poncho, shown here and detailed on pages 44 and 45, is a project that could have easily grown from a scarf.

Sprinkled throughout the book are subsections with instructions for making some of the projects into ponchos, so you have the opportunity to make a poncho rather than a scarf or a wrap if you choose.

Today's Novelty Yarns

Novelty yarn is any type of yarn that transcends the idea of a traditional basic yarn. Yarn has come a long way from being simply a choice between wool and cotton, or wool and acrylic.

Novelty yarn once meant merely the uneven thick and thin woolen handspun yarns, but today, an explosion of wonderful experimentation by the yarn companies has resulted in all possible combinations of synthetic and natural fibers, giving fiber crafters and artists an ever-growing source to express themselves creatively. Now you face a myriad of choices that include whether to use long, hairy eyelash yarn or thin threads spaced with sequins or tufts of color.

Yarn thickness has also taken a turn, with choices between super-thick roving to fluffy thick-and-thin wool to the straight-and-narrow parallel threads joined at intervals called railroad yarn. What makes these yarns so fun is that you knit with most of them on large needles so that the knitting works up very quickly, and you can turn out a colorful textured scarf in an afternoon. Even the thinner yarns work up wonderfully on thick needles, creating a fluid drape that was not the norm in knitwear in previous years.

Novelty yarn is a growing class of textured yarn that is constantly being added to with each season. Following are a few of the common terms used for describing some of these types of yarn currently on the market, as well as a few terms I have given to types of yarn that call for a category all their own.

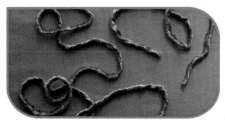

Novelty yarn: Any yarn that is differently textured than basic, standard traditional knitting yarn.

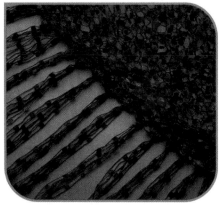

Novelty yarn.

Chenille: A fuzzy, velvety yarn that can be from about ⅛" thick to almost ½" thick. The yarn and finished knitting has a rich velour sheen and texture.

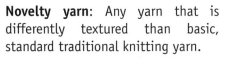

Chenille.

Eyelash: A thin strand of cord with long, usually between ½" to 1", strands hanging from the cord. The strands can be spaced at intervals, which creates little tufts of color in the knitting, or they can span the whole length of cord, which creates a fur fabric when knitted.

Eyelash yarns.

Fluffy: (This is my term.) This yarn is characterized by incredibly soft fiber, which feels like soft stuffing made into yarn. It consists of a thin cord that holds the fluffy stuff together.

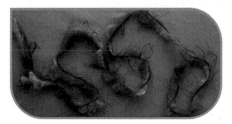

Fluffy yarn.

Metallic: Many types of yarn are enhanced by with a little sparkle, from a thin strand of silver- or gold-colored thread woven in with the main yarn to wisps of metallic eyelash spaced throughout the yarn.

Metallic yarns.

Mixes: A combination of different fiber types is the basis of most novelty yarns. It is a common yarn-making technique to blend the qualities of individual fibers in the finished yarn by mixing the fibers before the yarn is made, so that it looks like one fiber when spun into yarn. To add texture to a yarn though, two different types of finished yarn can be twisted together as in the bulky yarns shown. Another technique is to simply wind two different types of finished yarn into the same skein so it is just as if you chose two different yarns to knit together as one.

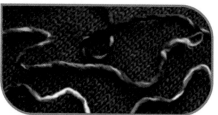

Bulky mix of two yarns twisted together as one.

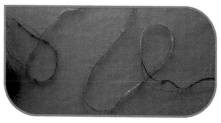

Yarn mix of two different yarns on the same skein.

Mohair: This yarn isn't new, and it's not really a novelty yarn, but it is different from the traditional idea of yarn and has some nice properties that go well with the novelty yarns listed here. It is often mixed with synthetic fibers to create some of the beautiful novelty yarns available. Mohair is characterized by a wispy halo of fibers that radiate out from a central core yarn, which can be thick, airy yarn or a thin, lace yarn, depending on the spinning process. Looped mohair is spaced with loops all along its length and doesn't have as much of a halo of fibers as basic mohair.

Mohair.

Railroad: Two thin cords with regularly spaced patches of fiber between them that holds them parallel to each other, usually between ⅛" and ¼" apart.

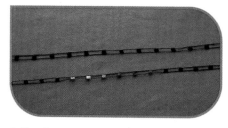

Railroad yarns.

Ribbon: Any flat ribbon-like material, usually from ⅛" to almost 1" wide.

Ribbon.

Roving: Thick (¼" to ½" wide) wool fibers in a rope form.

Roving yarn.

Spaced accents: (This is my term.) These are any "yarns" that are usually thin cords or even threads with tufts of color incorporated at spaced intervals throughout the length of the yarn. The accents can be anything from little pompoms to sequins to single eyelash strands.

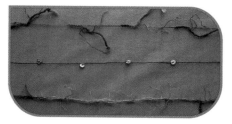

Spaced accent yarns.

Split-tufted railroad: (This is my term.) Thin cord with ¼"-long tufts of fiber at regular intervals. If you look at railroad yarn, then at this yarn, it looks as if one of the cords of the railroad yarn has been cut off to make this yarn.

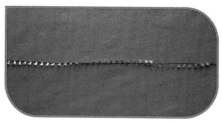

Split-tufted railroad yarn.

STANDARD YARN WEIGHT SYSTEM

Recently, yarn industry designers, manufacturers and publishers adopted a standardized system to help knitters understand the various yarn weights and needle sizes. These symbols, which appear on the yarn labels, are incorporated into each project in this book to make it easier for you to choose your own yarn variations. Use the chart as a guideline, as it reflects the most commonly used gauges and needle sizes for specific yarn categories.

YARN WEIGHT SYMBOL AND CATEGORY NAMES	SUPER FINE 1 SUPER FIN Super Fino	FINE 2 FIN Fino	LIGHT 3 LEGER Ligero	MEDIUM 4 MOYEN Medio	BULKY 5 BULKY Abultado	SUPER BULKY 6 SUPER BULKY Super Abultado
TYPES OF YARNS IN A CATEGORY	Sock, Fingering, Baby	Sport, Baby	DK, Light, Worsted	Worsted, Afghan, Aran	Chunky, Craft, Rug	Bulky, Roving
KNIT GAUGE RANGE IN ST ST TO 4"	27 to 32 sts	23 to 26 sts	21 to 24 sts	16 to 20 sts	12 to 15 sts	6 to 11 sts
RECOMMENDED METRIC NEEDLE SIZE RANGE	2.25mm to 3.25mm	3.25mm to 3.75mm	3.75mm to 4.5mm	4.5mm to 5.5mm	5.5mm to 8mm	8mm and larger
RECOMMENDED U.S. NEEDLE SIZE RANGE	#1 to #3	#3 to #5	#5 to #7	#7 to #9	#9 to #11	#11 and larger

SKILL LEVELS

A set of standard skill level icons also was introduced recently to the industry by the Craft Yarn Council of America. Each project in this book contains a skill level icon to guide you.

BEGINNER	Projects for first-time knitters, using basic knit and purl stitches and minimal shaping.
EASY	Projects using basic stitches, repetitive stitch patterns, simple color changes, and simple shaping and finishing.
INTERMEDIATE	Projects with a variety of stitches, such as basic cables and lace, simple intarsia, double-pointed needles and knitting in the round needle techniques, plus mid-level shaping and finishing.
EXPERIENCED	Projects using advance techniques and stitches, such as short rows, fair isle, more intricate intarsia, cables, lace patterns, plus numerous color changes.

WHAT THE YARN LABEL TELLS YOU

The label around your yarn contains several useful tidbits. Read the label carefully, as it divulges: yarn content; length of yarn in yards and meters; weight in ounces and grams; suggested knitting needle size and the resulting gauge; dye lot number; color name and number; and care instructions.

The care instructions are shown as symbols, as identified in the accompanying chart.

Additional symbols appear on labels to designate the various weights or thicknesses of yarns. A number from one to six is assigned, with one the finest weight and six the thickest (see Standard Yarn Weight Systems on page 13).

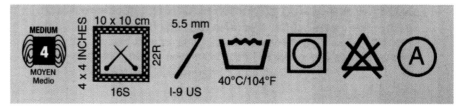

Washing		Pressing		Dry Cleaning	
⊠	Do not wash	⊠	Do not iron	⊠	Do not dry clean
	Hand-wash in warm water		Cool iron	Ⓐ	Dry cleanable in all solvents
30°	Hand-wash at temperature stated		Warm iron	Ⓕ	Dry cleanable with fluorocarbon or petroleum-based solvents only
	Machine wash		Hot iron	Ⓟ	Dry cleanable with perchlorethylene, hydrocarbons, or petroleum-based solvent
⊠	Do not tumble dry				
◯	Tumble drying acceptable				
−	Dry flat				
⊠	No bleach				
△	Chlorine bleach acceptable				

GAUGE

Checking the stitch gauge.

In most knitting, gauge is pretty cut and dry. You knit a swatch with the listed yarn and needle size, then you measure to see if it matches the row and stitch count shown in your pattern. If your gauge is too small (more stitches to the inch than needed), try another swatch with larger needles. If your gauge is too large (less stitches to the inch than needed), try another swatch with smaller needles.

It's a little more difficult to test gauge in the current knitting trend of larger needles because the knitting is so fluid and often obscured by fluff and fur. The gauge can be quite different, depending on whether the piece is hanging or lying flat on a table. Since these projects are meant to be worn so that they hang, most of the gauges are based on measuring when the scarf, wrap, shawl or poncho is hanging.

But since these aren't fitted clothing items, you really don't have to be too exact in your gauge. You just may end up with a scarf that is a little longer, shorter, wider or narrower than the "finished size" listed.

Checking gauge is often a trial-and-error process. If the gauge does not match the specs with a certain needle size, try one either smaller or larger for the desired result.

Knitting Abbreviations

If you are a beginner looking at knitting instructions for the first time, the abbreviations may seem a bit overwhelming. The following list is meant to help identify some of the more commonly used abbreviations in this book. In time and with practice, such knitting shorthand becomes second nature.

approx	approximately
b#	bead number (as explained in the Abbreviation Glossary, page 16)
beg	begin, beginning
BO	bind off
CO	cast on
ch	chain
cont	continue
dec	decrease - knit two together
dpn	double-pointed needle(s)
drp(#)	slide indicated number of yarn-overs off left needle
inc	increase - knit into the front and back of the stitch
K or k	knit
k2tog	knit two stitches together
LH	left hand
m	make one (as explained in the Abbreviation Glossary, page 16)
mm	millimeter(s)
oz	ounce(s)
P or p	purl
patt	pattern
pm	place marker
p2tog	purl two stitches together
rem	remain/remaining
rep	repeat(s)
RH	right hand
RS	right side
rnd(s)	round(s)
skp	slip one, knit one, pass slipped stitch over knit stitch
s2kp	slip two together as one, knit one, pass two slipped stitches over knit stitch (as explained in the Abbreviation Glossary, page 16)
sl	slip
sl st	slip stitch
st(s)	stitch(es)
St st	stockinette stitch
tog	together
yd	yard(s)
yo	yarn-over
**	repeat directions between asterisks
()	repeat directions between parentheses the number of times indicated
(#)lx(#)	left cross (as explained in the Abbreviation Glossary, page 17)
(#)rx(#)	right cross (as explained in the Abbreviation Glossary, page 17)

ABBREVIATION GLOSSARY

m (make one): Creates an extra stitch between stitches.

1. Lift the horizontal strand of yarn between the needles with the right needle before the next stitch, as in Figure 1-5.

2. Place the lifted stitch on the left needle, as in Figure 1-6.

3. Knit into the back of the strand.

s2kp (slip two, knit one, pass the two slipped stitches over)
Decreases two stitches, centering the middle stitch between the decreases.

1. Slip the next two stitches as one, inserting the needle knitwise into both stitches, as in Figure 1-7.

2. Knit the next stitch, as in Figure 1-8.

3. Pass the two slipped stitches as one over the knit stitch, as in Figures 1-9A and 1-9B.

b# (bead number): Designates the number of beads needed for a stitch.

1. Slide the specified number of beads up to the needle.

2. Work the next stitch indicated, so the beads are sitting between the stitch before and the stitch after the b# instruction.

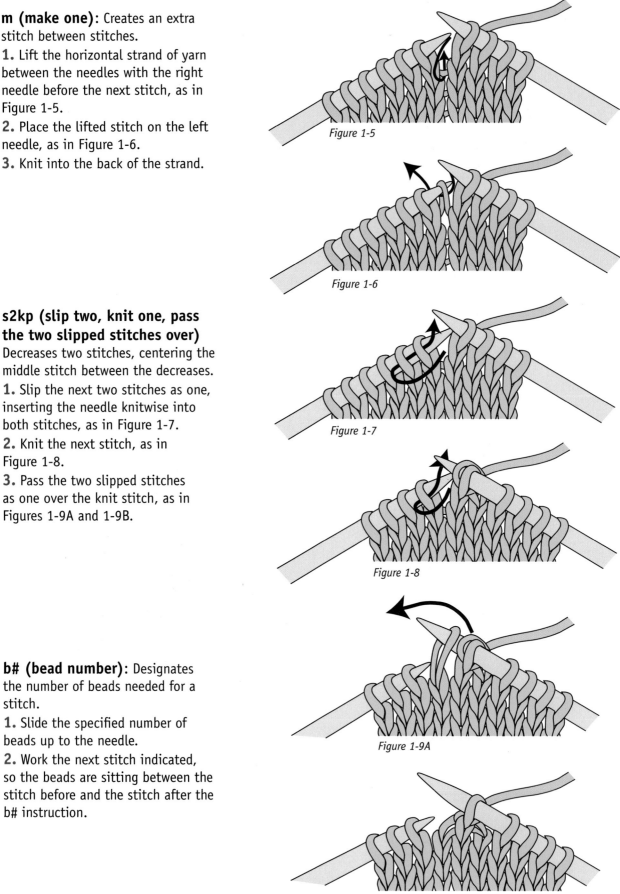

Figure 1-5

Figure 1-6

Figure 1-7

Figure 1-8

Figure 1-9A

Figure 1-9B

yo (yarn over): Technique for making lace, eyelets or long stitches.

1. Wrap the yarn around the needle before you work your next stitch, as in Figure 1-10.

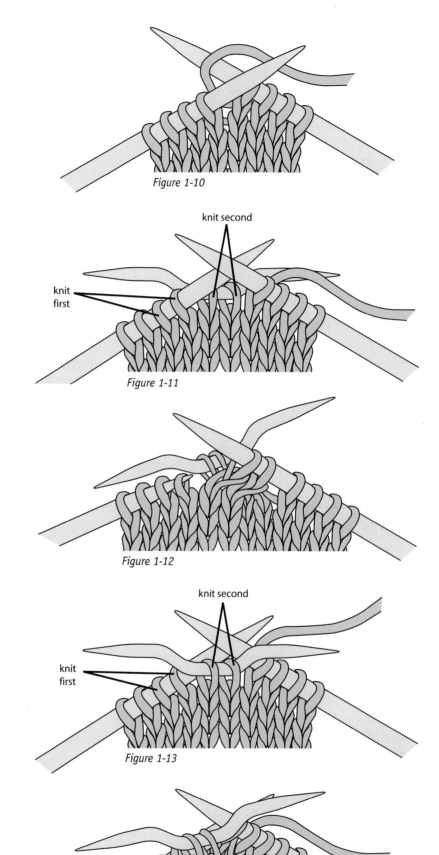

Figure 1-10

(#)rx(#) (right cross): Using a cable needle to twist the first stitch or stitches over and behind the next stitch or stitches.

1. Move the next stitch or stitches (indicated by the first number in parentheses) to the cable needle in back of the knitting, as in Figure 1-11.

2. Knit the next stitch or stitches (indicated by the last number in parentheses).

3. Knit the stitch or stitches from the cable needle, as in Figure 1-12.

knit second

knit first

Figure 1-11

Figure 1-12

(#)lx(#) (left cross): Using a cable needle to twist the first stitch or stitches (the first number in parenthesis) over in front of the next stitch or stitches(the last number in parenthesis).

1. Move the next stitch or stitches (indicated by the first number in parentheses) to the cable needle in front of the knitting, as in Figure 1-13.

2. Knit the next stitch or stitches (indicated by the last number in parentheses).

3. Knit the stitch or stitches from the cable needle, as in Figure 1-14.

knit second

knit first

Figure 1-13

Figure 1-14

Knitting Needles

Needles come in a variety of sizes, types and lengths and many different materials, including aluminum, plastic, wood and bamboo.

Knitting Needles Conversion

Here is a common conversion chart for U.S. and metric needle sizes, though you will occasionally find some variances in conversions.

U.S.	Metric (mm)
0	2.00
1	2.25
2	2.75
-	3.00
3	3.25
4	3.50
5	3.75
-	4.00
6	4.25
7	4.50
8	5.00
-	5.25
9	5.50
-	5.75
10	6.00
10½	6.50
-	7.00
-	7.50
11	8.00
13	9.00
15	10.00
17	12.75
19	15.00
35	19.00

Basic straight needles: These are pointed on one end, come in 10" and 14" lengths and are sold in pairs. Standard U.S. sizes range from 0 to 15 with some additional larger sizes for bulkier yarns. Many needles have both the U.S. sizes and the diameter in millimeters.

Circular needles: These are used to knit projects in a tube without creating a seam, or when making a very large project that doesn't easily fit on the straight needles.

Double-pointed needles: These are sold in sets of four or five and are used to make small, round projects, or to begin or end circular projects such as hats or cuffs of sleeves.

Flex needles: Straight single-point needles sold in pairs with a firm portion for forming the stitch and a flexible nylon shaft that allows much wider work to be held on the needles.

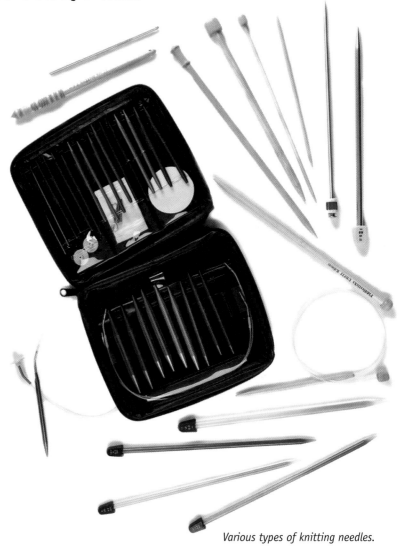

Various types of knitting needles.

OTHER KNITTING TOOLS

While the yarn and needles are the most basic of tools needed, you may consider also adding the following list of specialty items to your knitting basket.

Cable needles: Used to make cables.

Crochet hooks: Used to pick up dropped stitches and to add crocheted edgings.

Large-head pins: Used to pin knitted pieces together for sewing.

Point protectors: Used to protect the ends of needles and keep stitches from slipping off the needles between knitting sessions.

Row counters: Used to track the number of rows knitted when working patterns.

Stitch gauge: Used to measure knitting gauge.

Stitch holders: Used to hold part of the stitches while you knit a different part.

Stitch markers: Used to mark increases, decreases and pattern changes.

Yarn needle or **large-sized tapestry needle**: Used to seam finished pieces together or weave in yarn ends.

In addition to the special knitting tools, a good pair of sharp **scissors**, a **measuring tape** and an **iron** should also be on hand.

Basic Knitting Techniques and Terms

The following are some techniques and terms that will help you better understand some of the instructions used for the projects in this book.

CASTING ON (LONG TAIL)

To start a row of knitting, you need to get the yarn on the needle with the intended number of stitches. There are several methods used to cast on. This long tail method is the way I begin most of my knitting projects when I don't need to knit from the beginning stitches again.

1. Make a slipknot with a tail about three times as long as you want the width of your knitting to be and slide it onto the needle.

2. Hold the needle in your right hand and wrap the tail end of the yarn around your left thumb and the working end of the yarn around your left pointer finger, holding the ends of both yarns together with your other left-hand fingers.

3. Pass the right-hand needle under the strand over your thumb and then over the strand on your pointer finger, pulling through the opening created in the strands on your thumb, as in Figure 1-15.

4. Let the loop fall from your thumb and use your thumb to tighten the stitch on the needle, then position the strand of yarn back on your thumb as in Figure 1-15.

5. Repeat the process until you have the desired number of stitches on the needle (including the slipknot as a stitch).

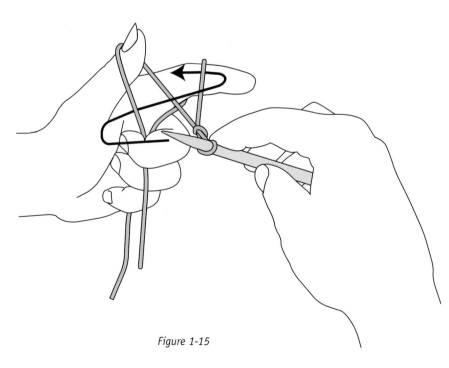

Figure 1-15

KNIT STITCH

One of two basic stitches, the knit stitch is essential in doing any knitting project.

1. Insert the right needle into the front of the first stitch on the left needle, from front to back, as in Figure 1-16. This is called "knitwise."

2. Wrap the yarn around the right needle counterclockwise, as in Figure 1-17.

3. Pull the wrapped yarn through the stitch on the left needle, sliding the old stitch off the left needle, creating a new stitch on the right needle, as in Figure 1-18.

4. Repeat steps 1 through 3 for each stitch on the left needle, until all are on the right.

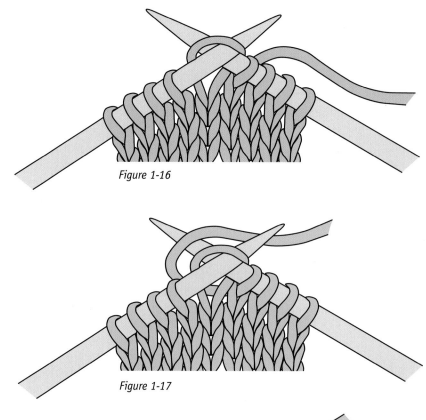

Figure 1-16

Figure 1-17

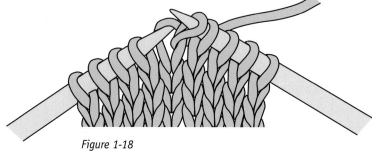

Figure 1-18

ADDING A NEW YARN

When you get to the last 12" or so of your working yarn, you will need to add a new ball of yarn.

1. Hold the end of the working yarn and the tail of the new yarn together as one and tie an overhand knot, as in Figure 1-19, leaving about 4" of a tail for each yarn strand. Don't tie the knot tight.

2. Continue knitting until pattern is complete.

3. Go back and untie the overhand knot, thread one tail with a tapestry needle and weave the end into the fabric. Repeat for the other tail.

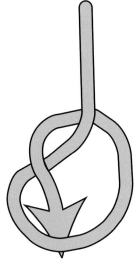

Figure 1-19

PURL STITCH

The purl stitch is the other of the basic knitting stitches.

1. Insert the right needle into the front of the first stitch on the left needle, from back to front, as in Figure 1-20. This is called "purlwise."

2. Wrap the yarn around the right needle counterclockwise, as in Figure 1-21.

3. Pull the wrapped yarn through the stitch on the left needle, sliding the old stitch off the left needle, creating a new stitch on the right needle, as in Figure 1-22.

4. Repeat steps 1 through 3 for each stitch on the left needle, until all are on the right.

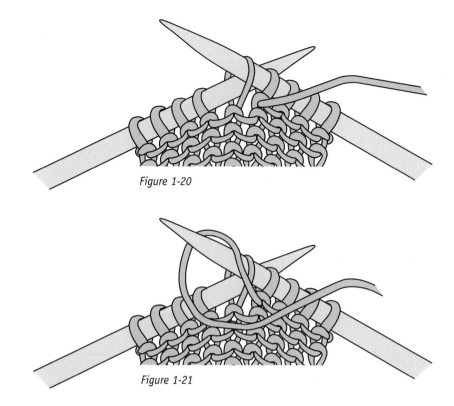

Figure 1-20

Figure 1-21

Figure 1-22

BINDING OFF

Binding off your stitches at the end of your work is necessary to keep the piece from unraveling.

1. Knit the first two stitches.

2. Pass the first stitch over the second stitch on the right needle, as in Figure 1-23.

3. Knit the next stitch.

4. Pass the first stitch on the right needle over the stitch just knitted.

5. Repeat steps 3 and 4 for each stitch across the row.

6. Cut the yarn and pass it through the last stitch to finish the row.

7. Weave in the tail.

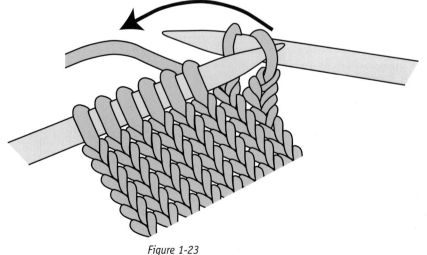

Figure 1-23

WEAVING IN TAIL

In most cases, to weave in loose ends of yarn in knitting, you don't want to make knots and you don't want the yarn to show on the right side of the fabric.

1. Thread the yarn tail with a tapestry needle and pass the yarn to the backside of the work if it isn't there already.

2. Pass under the bumps along one row of knitting, or follow the knit stitch, duplicating the path that the stitches made as you knitted them. Work the yarn in for about 1½", as in Figure 1-24.

3. Cut yarn close to the knitted fabric.

For some novelty yarns that are slippery or knitted on large needles where the finished knitted fabric is very loose, you can sometimes tie the ends in a square knot and cut them about ½" away from the knot. They will not show and will make a good strong ending for the yarn.

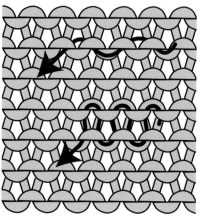

Figure 1-24

GRAFTING/JOINING

Grafting is the process of joining two pieces of knitting together that have "live stitches," meaning stitches that are still on the needle, rather than bound off. Grafting creates an invisible seam, since you are actually hand sewing a row of knitting, joining the two pieces together. This is a perfect join for a scarf that you begin at the ends and work toward the center.

In stockinette and garter stitches, you can make the join completely invisible, and in patterned stitches, it's usually half a stitch off.

1. Line up the two pieces to be joined so they are butted up against each other, right sides up, and still on the needles with the working end of yarn at your right.

2. Cut the working end of yarn of one of the pieces to three times the width of the piece and thread it with a blunt tapestry needle.

3. Pass through the first two stitches on the opposite piece, going in the first stitch from front to back and out the second stitch from back to front, dropping the first stitch off the knitting needle, as in Figure 1-25.

4. Pass through the first two stitches on the other needle in the same way, dropping the first stitch off the knitting needle, as in Figure 1-26.

5. Repeat steps 3 and 4 with the new first two stitches on each needle, each time pulling the stitches so they are the same tension as the rest of the knitting.

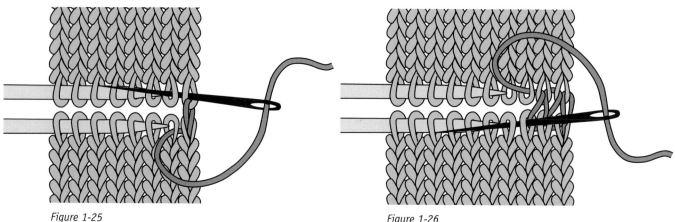

Figure 1-25   *Figure 1-26*

Specialty Stitches and Techniques

Here is a reference of individual stitch patterns used for projects throughout the book. Please refer to the actual project for the exact instructions.

CABLES

Cables are wonderful textured patterns that can range from a simple twist of a few stitches every few rows to a complex pattern of interwoven bands. To make a cable, you need a cable needle, which is a short double-ended needle sometimes with a small curve in the middle.

1. Cast on the number of stitches indicated in the pattern onto the cable needle.

2. Position the cable needle to the front or to the back of the knitting, as indicated in the pattern.

3. Work the next stitches from the left needle to the right needle and then the stitches from the cable needle. This process twists the order of the stitches, creating the overlapping columns of stitches.

Three examples of cable patterns.

DIAMOND PATTERN

This is a beautiful old pattern that I don't think is used often enough in knitting designs. It is basically garter stitch with many yarn-overs. It is worked by adding graduated numbers of yarn-overs between stitches on one row and then dropping them off the needle on the following row. The wonderful undulating pattern is created from the flow of elongated stitches to short stitches and back again.

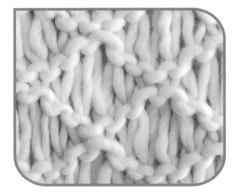

Example of diamond pattern.

EYELETS

Eyelets are a step between basic knitted fabric and lace. They add nice detail to an otherwise plain fabric, lightening the design, but not opening it up so much that it becomes lace. Like lace, eyelets are created by working yarn-overs and then balancing those with a decrease. This creates a small hole in the knitting, but doesn't change the overall number of stitches in the piece.

Example of eyelet pattern.

GARTER STITCH

Garter stitch is created when every row is made only of knit stitches. The resulting fabric has a horizontal stripe of bumps created from the backside of each knit row, showing on both sides of the fabric. It is a reversible pattern and is great for novelty yarn since it shows off the texture of the yarn.

Example of garter stitch pattern.

KNIT-PURL VARIATION

By playing with knit-purl patterns, you can come up with all sorts of different textures. This three-row repeat is easy to work and creates an interesting texture.

Example of knit-purl pattern.

I-CORD

I-cord is a great design tool that can be used for everything from the edging on a pillow to handles on a purse. It is usually made three to six stitches wide.

To make four-stitch I-cord:

1. Cast on four stitches, using double-pointed needles.
2. Knit across the row.
3. Slide the knitting to the other side of the needle, keeping the knitting facing you. (You don't turn and purl back the other way in I-cord.)
4. Pull the working yarn behind the knitting, as in Figure 1-27, and knit the four stitches again.
5. Repeat steps 3 and 4 for every row.

Figure 1-27

Example of I-cord pattern.

LACE

Lace is full of opportunity for making beautiful, delicate designs. It is amazing that so much can be achieved from yarn-overs, increases and simple decreases. From complex patterns that take patience and concentration to follow to simple small repeats, there is a full range of skill needed in lace-making.

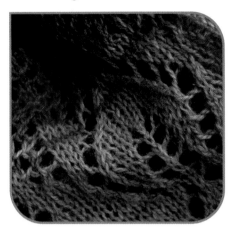

Example of lace pattern.

MOSS STITCH

Moss stitch is a four-row repeat of knit one, purl one. The basics of the pattern is to knit the knit stitch and purl the purl stitches for two rows. Then you switch and knit the purl stitches and purl the knit stitches on the next row. Continuing on the fourth row in the new pattern, knit the new knit stitches and purl the new purl stitches. Then begin the repeat by switching back to the first-row pattern.

Example of moss stitch pattern.

RIB STITCH

Rib stitch patterns are created when you knit one or more stitches, then purl one or more stitches on all right-side rows, and you purl the knit stitches and knit the purl stitches on the wrong-side rows. This makes vertical columns of texture with the knit stitches coming forward and the purl stitches pushing back on the knitted surface. The knit and purl sections can be the same or different numbers of stitches in each section.

Example of rib stitch pattern.

STOCKINETTE STITCH

Stockinette stitch is when you knit all the right-side rows and purl all the wrong-side rows. The front is smooth and the back has all the bumps.

Example of stockinette stitch pattern.

YARN-OVERS DROPPED OFF THE NEEDLE

This is a great stitch to show off novelty yarns that are large, like thick ribbons or wool roving. It is a modified garter stitch in which you work several rows of garter stitch. Then on the next row, work a yarn-over between each stitch (but not at the very end or beginning of the row). Then on the next row, knit the stitches and drop the yarn-overs off the needle. This stretches out the whole row.

Example of yarn-overs dropped off the needle pattern.

Knitting with Beads

When working with beads and yarn, there are several things to keep in mind.

Your first consideration is the yarn and beads. The beads need to have holes large enough to go onto the yarn, and the yarn needs to be strong enough to have the beads slide over it several times without breaking. The yarn also needs to be smooth enough so the beads don't get caught up in any slubs or uneven textures. It's a good idea to try some beads on the yarn you want to use and make a test swatch to see how you like the look of the beads and yarn together.

Another consideration is how you will work with all those beads strung onto the yarn. Here are some techniques to make it easier.

- The easiest way to get the beads onto the yarn is to tie a 12" piece of sewing or beading thread to the yarn about 3" from the tail, so the yarn is simply folded in half and the beads can be picked up with a beading needle and slid down the thread and onto the yarn.

- It's easier to keep the yarn and beads from tangling as you work if you place them in a bowl or basket and let the part of the yarn with beads on it pile loosely in the container. You will need to slide the beads up to the needle for knitting them into the work, or away from the needle to allow room to knit as you work on your piece.

- To slide the beads along the yarn, slide about 4" to 6" of beads at a time so you don't put too much wear and tear on the yarn.

- The number in parentheses at the beginning of each row is the number of beads needed for that row. If you slide that number of beads up to your working area and have about two feet of bare yarn before the rest of the beads, you will have enough yarn to knit the row, and you will be able to double-check that you knit the row accurately since you have the number of beads you need for that row already counted out and near the needle.

Easy Novelty Yarn Projects

Chapter 2

This chapter begins with a basic garter stitch scarf presented in different yarns and using varying numbers of stitches for each scarf. With a simple pattern of casting on less than 20 stitches and knitting each row, you can create a huge selection of looks just by changing the type of yarn used. But don't stop there! By just increasing one stitch each row, you can make a beautiful triangle shawl, or you can play with color to make stripes or combine yarns to create your own color/texture masterpiece!

Garter Stitch Scarves

You will find basic patterns like these garter stitch scarves everywhere, from the labels on the yarn you buy to the mail-order catalogs to yarn Internet sites. These three basic scarves demonstrate the range of simple garter stitch scarves.

AIRY JEWEL SCARF

BEGINNER

BULKY
5
BULKY
Abultado

This scarf contrasts the other two and shows how a more traditional "novelty" yarn handles in a basic garter stitch scarf pattern.

Finished Size
8" x 48"
Gauge
8 sts and 9 rows = 4"

MATERIALS
- 1 skein (120yd/110m) green/purple/ blue variegated mohair blend*
- Size 19 (15mm) needles

*Used in this project: 1 skein Lorna's Laces Glory (mohair blend, 120yds/110m), color #56 Mountain Creek.

INSTRUCTIONS
CO 16 sts.
K every row (garter st) until work measures 48".
BO and weave in ends.

GREEN GRASS BOA

To me, this scarf, knit in classic eyelash yarn, is the symbol of the new novelty yarn knitting. It works up fast on large needles and although all those loose "eyelashes" can be a bit of a nuisance while knitting, the finished project is so far from traditional knitting, it is a must-try for anyone who knits.

Finished Size
2" x 100"
Gauge
(Measure in garter stitch with scarf hanging.)
20 sts and 7 rows = 4"

MATERIALS
· 2 skeins (51yd/47m) ¾"-long classic eyelash yarn*
· Size 17 (12.75mm) needles

*Used in this project: 2 skeins Artful Yarns' Galaxy (62% nylon/38% polyester, 51yds/47m, 1.75oz/50g), color #282.

INSTRUCTIONS
CO 10 sts.
K every row (garter st) until work measures 100".
BO and weave in ends.

RAINBOW LINGERIE RIBBON ASCOT

This variation is an easy and quick project that demonstrates using just one skein of a special yarn to make a fine little scarf.

Finished Size
3" x 38"
Gauge
16 sts and 16 rows = 4"

MATERIALS
· 1 skein rainbow variegated ribbon*
· Size 11 (8mm) needles

*Used in this project: 1 skein hand-dyed synthetic ribbon.

INSTRUCTIONS
CO 12 sts.
K every row (garter st) until work measures 38".
BO and weave in ends.

Tapered Ascot

EASY

BULKY 5
BULKY
Abultado

An easy way to add a little change to your next scarf is to make it with tapered ends, which are great for small little accent scarves like this garter stitch ascot. Choose the yarn shown for a casual blue jean companion or go dressy with something more silky. With so many types of yarn to choose from, you could have one for each day!

Finished Size
4" x 40"
Gauge
14 sts and 12 rows = 4"

MATERIALS
· 1 ball (60.5yd/55m) bulky weight novelty yarn*
· Size 13 (9mm) needles

*Used in this project: 1 ball Filatura Di Crosa's Hopla (100% polyester, 65.5yd/55m, 1.75oz/50g), color #11.

INSTRUCTIONS
CO 1 st.
Row 1: Inc 1 - 2 sts.
Row 2: Inc, k1 - 3 sts.
Row 3: Inc, k2 - 4 sts.
Row 4: Inc, k rem sts - 5 sts.
Rep row 4 until there are 14 sts.
Cont in garter st until work is 35".
Dec 1 st at beg of each row until 2 sts are left.
Pass yarn through last 2 sts and weave in ends.

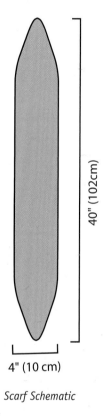

40" (102cm)

4" (10 cm)

Scarf Schematic

Garter Stitch Loopy Mohair Shawl

EASY

BULKY 5 BULKY Abultado

If you are ready to try a larger project than a simple scarf, but want to keep working in garter stitch and novelty yarn, here is the project for you. This is a great first shawl because it is easy to knit on the large needles, and the finished piece looks beautiful in the loopy mohair yarn, with the long brushed mohair fringe. It's reversible in garter stitch, and feels warm and airy in the soft light mohair.

Finished Size
50" x 38",
not including 7½" fringe
Gauge
9 sts and 11 rows = 4"

MATERIALS
· 3 skeins (75yd/69m) mohair loop yarn*
· 2 skeins (125yd/115m) brushed mohair yarn*
· Size 17 (1.75mm) needle
· Size N (10mm) crochet hook

*Used in this project: 3 skeins Ironstone Yarns' Bouquet of Colors Mohair/Loop (90% mohair/5% wool/5% nylon, 75yd/69m, 2oz/56g), color #5011 Mountain Grass, and 2 skeins Ironstone Yarns' Bouquet of Colors Mohair/Brushed (78% mohair/13% wool/9% nylon, 125yd/115m, 2oz/56g), color #5013 Seaside.

INSTRUCTIONS
CO 1 st with mohair loop yarn.
Row 1: Inc 1 - 2 sts.
Row 2: Inc 1, k1 - 3 sts.
Row 4: Inc 1, k rem sts - 4 sts.
Rep row 4 until work is 38".
BO and weave in ends.

FRINGE
Using the brushed mohair yarn,
1. Cut 216 15" lengths of brushed mohair yarn.
2. Group the cut lengths in sets of three.
3. Fold each group of three strands in half.
4. Use crochet hook to attach them along the sides and bottom point of the shawl, spacing them about 1½" apart.
5. Add more, if needed.

PONCHO VARIATION
You will need twice as much yarn for a poncho as you needed for the shawl.
1. Follow the shawl instructions, using two skeins of the looped mohair and then repeat with two more skeins of looped mohair for two complete shawls.
2. Pin the two pieces together and try it on to see how big of a neck opening you will need (typically 12" to 14").
3. Sew the top edges together, leaving a 12" to 14" opening in the middle for the neck opening.
4. Fringe the poncho the same as for the shawl.

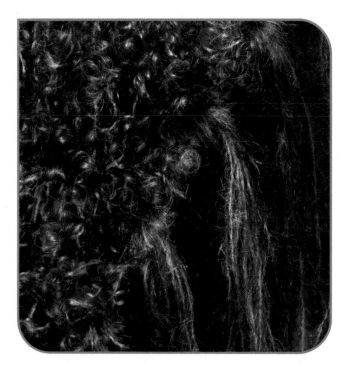

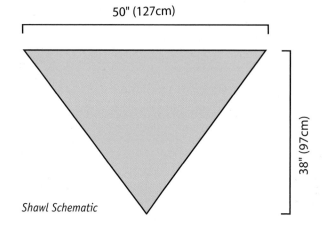

50" (127cm)

38" (97cm)

Shawl Schematic

Fringed Scarf/Beach Skirt

BEGINNER

This lusciously drapy scarf/skirt shows how knitting with large needles and thin-textured yarn can create a fluid, textured fabric that nobody had done in knitting until the last several years. This long fringed piece is easy to make in simple garter stitch, and doubles as a beach skirt wonderfully, making it an ideal accessory to take on vacations. Wear it over your bikini or T-shirt at the beach. Then, as the sun sets, magically transform yourself by wearing it over an elegant evening gown at dinner.

Finished Size
82" x 26",
not including 7" fringe
Gauge
7½ sts and 9½ rows = 4"

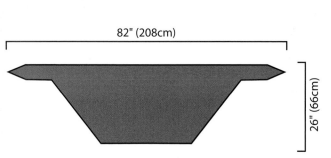

82" (208cm)

26" (66cm)

Scarf/Skirt Schematic

MATERIALS
· 5 balls (82yd/75m) railroad novelty yarn in variegated reds*
· Size 11 (8mm) needles
· Size I (5.5mm) crochet hook
· Stitch marker

*Used in this project: 5 balls Trendsetter's Binario
(100% polyester, 82yd/75m, .9oz/25g), color #103.

INSTRUCTIONS
CO 1 st.
Row 1: Inc 1 - 2 sts.
Row 2: Inc 1, k1 - 3 sts.
Row 3: Inc 1, k rem sts - 4 sts.
Rep row 3 until there are 18 sts.
Work even in garter st for 20 rows.
Pm at one side edge. This will be the fringe side of
  the scarf.
Inc 1 st at beg of each row on the side with the stitch
    marker until there are 50 sts.
Work even for 60 more rows.
Dec 1 st at beg of each row on the side with the
  stitch marker until there are 18 sts.
Work even for 20 rows.
Dec 1 st at beg of each row until 2 sts are left.
BO through both sts and weave in ends.

FRINGE
1. Hold two strands of yarn together as one and cut
76 14" lengths.
2. Keep in groups of two.
3. Fold each group of two strands in half.
4. Use crochet hook to attach them along the bottom
edge, beginning about 16" from one of the pointed
ends of the scarf.
5. Attach more or fewer lengths as needed to reach
16" from the other end of the scarf.

Teal and Railroad Long-Stripe Scarf

This scarf project is basically the same as the Spring Green Short-Stripe Scarf that follows it; cast on the number of stitches and work in garter stitch, changing colors every few rows to create your design. Yet these examples show how the yarn and direction of the stripe can have a huge effect on the project, as this scarf is more elegant and flowing, while the other is more furry and fluffy. For this project, using the large needles to cast on ensures that both sides of the scarf will have similar tension.

EASY

MEDIUM
4
MOYEN
Medio

Finished Size
3½" x 90",
not including 8" fringe
Gauge
6½ sts and 27 rows = 4"

MATERIALS
· 1 skein (82yd/76m) worsted weight teal yarn*
· 1 ball (78yd/72m) railroad rainbow variegated yarn*
· Size 15 (10mm) 32"-long circular needles
· Size 13 (10mm) 32"-long circular needles
· Size I (5.5mm) crochet hook

*Used in this project: 1 skein Berroco's Quest
(100% nylon, 82yd/76m, 1.75oz/50g), color #9823, and 1 ball
Berroco's Mosaic FX (100% nylon, 78yd/72m, .875oz/25g), color #4615.

INSTRUCTIONS
CO 150 sts, using the larger needles and the teal yarn.
Change to the smaller needles and k 2 rows.
Change to railroad yarn and k 4 rows.
Change to teal and k 4 rows.
Rep k 4 rows in railroad, then k 4 rows in teal.
K 4 rows in railroad, then k 2 rows in teal.
BO loosely in teal and weave in ends.

FRINGE
1. Hold both yarns together as one and cut 24 pairs of 16" lengths of yarn.
2. Fold each pair of the 16" strands in half.
3. Use crochet hook to attach one pair to the end of each row.
4. Cut the fringe ends so they are even.

Spring Green Short-Stripe Scarf

As noted in the Teal and Railroad Long-Stripe Scarf, this scarf is basically worked the same way, but oh what a difference the yarn choice makes! This scarf with its bright colors and funky textured yarn is bold, bright and fun—far less formal than the long-stripe variation. This patterning of yarn opens up the possibilities of design with all the wonderful textures of novelty yarn available.

EASY

BULKY
5
BULKY
Abultado

Finished Size
4½" x 54", not including 10" fringe
Gauge
15 sts and 5½ rows = 4"

MATERIALS
· 1 ball (85yd/78m) chartreuse furry novelty yarn*
· 1 ball (100yd/92m) thin novelty yarn with tufts of color in purple, blue and green spaced about 1½" to 2" apart*
· Size 19 (15mm) needles
· Size N (10mm) crochet hook

*Used in this project: 1 ball Crystal Palace Yarns' Squiggle (50% nylon/50% polyester, 100yd/92m, 1.75oz/50g), color #9289, and 1 ball Crystal Palace Yarns' Splash (100% polyester, 85yd/78m, 3.5oz/100g), color #7191.

INSTRUCTIONS
CO 17 sts with furry chartreuse novelty yarn.
K 3 rows.
K 2 rows in thin multicolored novelty yarn and 4 rows in chartreuse, rep 11 times.
K 2 rows multi.
K 3 rows chartreuse.
BO loosely and weave in ends.

FRINGE
1. Cut 32 20" lengths of chartreuse yarn.
2. Fold each 20" strand in half.
3. Use crochet hook to attach each along scarf ends between each stitch.

Purple Ribbon Condo Knit Mini Scarf

"Condo" knitting was a term that surfaced for a short time in knitting magazines in the '80s. It's an easy way to work up projects faster. It mimics the technique of wrapping yarn around the needle in one row and then dropping the wrap off the needle in the next row, which is the technique used in the Golden Dropped-Stitch Scarf on pages 42 and 43 and the Winter White Two-Pattern Scarf on pages 60 to 62. To condo knit, you simply work some rows with very large needles and others with small needles. This creates a pattern of elongated stitches and short stitches.

EASY

BULKY 5 BULKY Abultado

Finished Size
2" x 45", not including 9" fringe
Gauge
(Measure in garter stitch with size 11 needles.)
18 sts and 17 rows = 4"

MATERIALS

- 1 hank (75yd/68m) ³⁄₈"-wide two-toned purple ribbon*
- Size 11 (8mm) needles
- Size 19 (15mm) needles
- Size I (5.5mm) crochet hook

*Used in this project: 1 hank Knit One Crochet Too's Tartelette (50% cotton/40% tactel nylon/10% nylon, 75yd/68m, 1.75oz/50g), color #719.

TIP:
When you change to the different-sized needles, in your first row of knitting with the new size needle, you are actually working with both sizes at one time. The left hand has all the stitches from the previous row on the first size needles, while the right hand holds the new size needle to knit the stitches.

INSTRUCTIONS

CO 9 sts with size 11 needles.
K 5 rows with size 11 needles and k 5 rows with size 19 needles; rep 9 times.
K 5 rows with size 11 needles.
BO and weave in ends.

FRINGE

1. Cut 18 18" lengths of ribbon.
2. Fold each 18" strand in half.
3. Use crochet hook to attach each along scarf ends into each stitch.
4. Trim the fringe ends so they are equal in length.

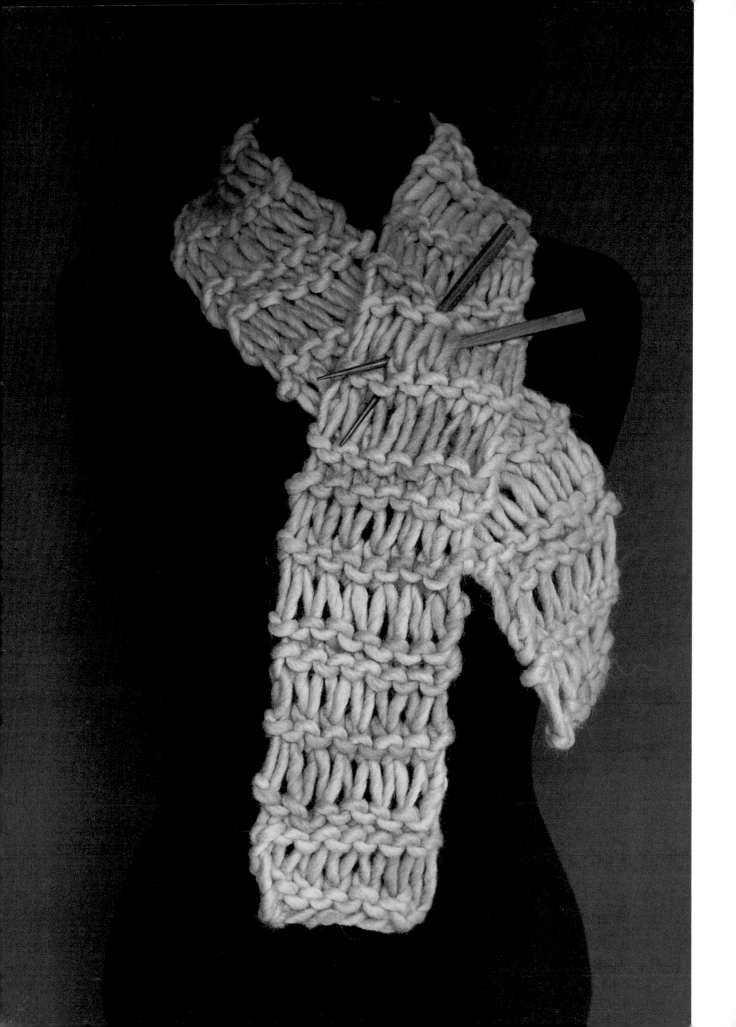

Golden Dropped-Stitch Scarf

EASY

SUPER BULKY
6
SUPER BULKY
Super Abultado

This is the "other" way of creating elongated rows of stitches. It is a great technique for super bulky yarn, since it creates less bulk, and you wouldn't be able to find a big enough needle to use the condo technique. It's also an excellent way to show off wide, textured ribbons or any yarn that is just as beautiful in long straight lengths as it is knitted. Unlike the condo knitting technique where you simply use different-sized needles, here you work yarn-overs between each stitch on one row and then drop the yarn-overs off the needle on the next row. This creates the long stretches of yarn on these rows. By working some rows with the dropped stitches and others without, you can create different patterns. The knitting goes fast and the design is different from basic garter stitch.

Finished Size
4" x 48"
Gauge
(Measure in garter stitch.)
7 sts and 5 rows = 4"

MATERIALS

· 1 skein (45yd/42m) super bulky gold roving yarn*
· Size 35 (19mm) needles

*Used in this project: 1 skein Blue Sky Alpacas' Bulky Hand Dyes (50% alpaca/50% wool, 45yd/42m, 3.5oz/100g), color #1016 Yellow.

INSTRUCTIONS

CO 7 sts.
Row 1: K.
Row 2: (K1 yo) 6 times, k1.
Row 3: (K1, drop yo off needle) 6 times, k1.
Row 4: K.
Rep rows 2 through 4 until 48".
BO and weave in ends.

Bold Stripes Serape-Style Poncho

This bold poncho exemplifies all that is new in knitting, from the poncho design to the use of the fuzzy novelty yarn stripes. The fluid drape created by using large needles is also a recent knitting technique that makes a traditionally stiff design hang gracefully off the shoulders. Make it short and wide as shown, or knit it longer before and after the neck opening to create a longer covering.

EASY

MEDIUM
4
MOYEN
Medio

Finished Size
48" from beginning to end and 52" across from wrist to wrist
Gauge
7 sts and 11 rows = 4"

MATERIALS
- 6 balls (163yd/150m) medium-weight brown yarn*
- 2 balls (47yd/43m) medium-weight beige novelty yarn*
- Size 17 (12.75mm) 32" or 36" circular needles

*Used for this project: 6 balls Patons' Katrina (92% rayon/8% polyester, 163yd/150m, 3.5oz/100g), color #10031 Chocolate, and 2 balls Patons' Allure (100% nylon, 47yd/43m, 1.75oz/50g), color #04011 Sable.

INSTRUCTIONS
CO 90 sts in beige novelty yarn.
K 2 rows.
K 6 rows in brown yarn and 2 rows in beige; rep twice.
K 40 rows in brown.

Neckline
K 35 sts at beg of next row.
BO the next 20 sts.
K rem 35 sts to end of row.

Shoulders
K 4 rows, working the shoulders separately.
On next row, beg at outer end of shoulder, k 35 sts of that shoulder side.
CO 20 sts for back of the neck opening.
K 35 sts of other shoulder.
Now beg working across one shoulder, the neck opening and the other shoulder - 90 sts.
K 40 rows in brown.
K 2 rows in beige and 6 rows in brown yarn; rep twice.
K 2 rows in beige.
BO and weave in ends.

Combined Yarns Scarves

Now that you have spent some time knitting with the great new yarns available, it's time to have some fun blending yarns together to create your very own color and texture. It's easy, because all you do is pick two or more yarns and hold them together as one while you knit in garter stitch. The knitting goes quickly, too, since you usually need a larger needle than what you would use with one strand of yarn. You might also be surprised by the new color you create by pairing some very different yarns together.

This technique is a great way to use up odd lots of yarn from other projects. Gather all your odd balls of yarn and blend them together as you knit, changing colors as the yarn gets used up. You will end up with a multitextured, multicolored scarf that is different at each end. A bohemian treasure!

SLINKY NEUTRALS SCARF

EASY

Finished Size
4½" x 44"
Gauge
21 sts and 12 rows = 4"

LIGHT
3
LEGER Ligero

Split-tufted Railroad Yarn

FINE
2
FIN Fino

Sparse Eyelash Yarn

MATERIALS

· 1 ball (125yd/115m) split-tufted railroad yarn*
· 1 ball (200yd/185m) sparse eyelash*
· Size 13 (9mm) needles

*Used in this project: 1 ball Plymouth Yarn's Electra (100% nylon, 125yd/115m, 1.75oz/50g), color #01, and 1 ball Plymouth Yarn's Whisper (100% nylon, 200yd/185m, 1.75oz/50g), color #23.

INSTRUCTIONS

Hold both yarns tog as 1 and CO 24 sts.
Work in garter st until 44" or desired length.
BO loosely and weave in ends.

GOLD AND EARTH FRINGED SCARF

Finished Size
3½" x 46", not including 4" fringe
Gauge
17 sts and 10 rows = 4"

EASY

Lightweight Yarn

Metallic Cord

MATERIALS
- 1 ball (93yd/88m) lightweight yarn with small tufts every 2"*
- 1 cone (108yd/100m) metallic gold cord*
- Size 15 (10mm) needles
- Size H (5mm) crochet hook

*Used in this project: 1 ball Plymouth Yarn's Flirt (100% nylon, 93yd/88m, 1.75oz/50g), color #103, and 1 cone Plymouth Yarn's Gold Rush (80% rayon/20% metallised polyester, 108yd/100m, .9oz/25g), color #1.

INSTRUCTIONS
Hold 2 yarns tog as 1 and CO 15 sts.
Work in garter st until 46".
BO and weave in ends.

FRINGE
1. Hold both yarns together as one and cut 30 8" lengths of yarn.
2. Fold each two-strand group in half.
3. Use crochet hook to attach each group along scarf ends into each stitch.

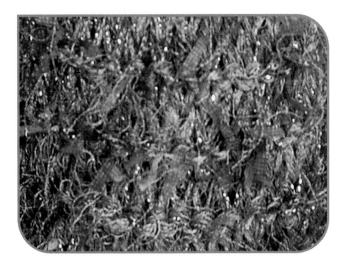

COPPER AND SEQUINS FRINGED SCARF

Finished Size
4" x 52", not including 8" fringe
Gauge
10 sts and 7 rows = 4"

Worsted-weight   Bulky/Furry Variegated Yarn   Sequins Yarn

MATERIALS
- 1 ball (82yd/76m) worsted-weight copper-colored yarn*
- 1 ball (55yd/50m) bulky yarn with furry texture and variegated browns and black*
- 1 ball (70yd/64m) thin yarn with gold sequins spaced about 2" apart*
- Size 19 (15mm) needles
- Size I (5.5mm) crochet hook

*Used in this project: 1 ball each Berroco's Lavish (40% nylon/32% wool/15% polyester/13% acrylic, 55yd/50m, 1.75oz/50g), color #7324; Berroco's Quest (100% nylon, 82yd/76m, 1.75oz/50g), color #9813, and Berroco's Lazer FX (100% polyester, 70yd/64m, .35oz/10g), color #6004.

INSTRUCTIONS
Hold the 3 different yarns tog as 1 and CO 10 sts.
Work in garter st for 30 rows.
Drop the sequin yarn and cont k for 30 rows.
Add the sequin yarn back in and k for 30 more rows.
BO and weave in ends.

FRINGE
1. Hold all three yarns together as one and cut 20 16" lengths of yarn.
2. Fold each three-strand group in half.
3. Use crochet hook to attach each group along scarf ends into each stitch.
4. Trim the fringe ends so they are equal in length.

Knit and Purl Projects

Chapter 3

These projects use easy knit and purl stitches to make everything from a small simple ascot to an elegant poncho. The yarn ranges from basic, traditional wool yarn to fun novelty yarns of thick wool roving and sparkly fur textures. The basic stockinette stitch projects use several types of yarn, but the projects with stitch patterns look best in traditional yarns that don't compete with the pattern.

Lavish Wrap

BEGINNER

BULKY
5
BULKY
Abultado

This fabulous wrap exemplifies the beauty of the yarns available today. By just knitting a rectangle in stockinette stitch, you create a luxurious wrap that is soft and warm with just the right touch of sparkle. It's a joy to be able to make something so beautiful and useful, with such ease. And it's all because of the yarn!

Finished Size
30" x 60"
Gauge
10 sts and 12 rows = 4"

MATERIALS

· 12 balls (55yd/50m) bulky-weight yarn
  with furry texture and variegated browns and black*
· Size 13 (9mm) needles

*Used in this project: 12 balls Berroco's Lavish (40% nylon/32% wool/
15% polyester/13% acrylic, 55yd/50m, 1.75oz/50g), color #7324.

INSTRUCTIONS

CO 75 sts.
Work in St st until 60".
BO and weave in ends.

Poncho Variation
You will need about 7 balls of yarn to make a poncho.
CO 34 sts.
Work in St st until 33" long.
BO and weave in ends.
Rep for 2 rectangles.
Sew the rectangles tog as in the Easy Evening Poncho
 on page 53.

Easy Evening Poncho

EASY

SUPER FINE
1
SUPER FIN
Super Fino

Ponchos have come a long way from those clunky crocheted items of the '60s. This one is light and airy because you use big needles to knit the thin, mixed-metallic yarn. The result is a fabric with a hint of transparency that drapes elegantly over your outfit. The two easy-to-knit rectangles are quickly sewn together, and then you are done! Unless you choose to add fringe or beading along the edge...

Finished Size
30" circumference neck opening
25" from neckline to center front or back point
14" from neckline to arm edge.
Made from two 14" x 33" rectangles
Gauge
(Measure in stockinette stitch.)
14 sts and 18 rows = 4"

MATERIALS

· 3 balls (198yd/180m) variegated red metallic fingering yarn*
· Size 10 (6mm) needles
· Size F (3.75mm) crochet hook

*Used in this project: 3 skeins S. Charles' Ritratto (28% mohair/53% rayon/ 10% nylon/9% polyester, 198yd/180m, 1.75oz/50g), color #73 Red.

INSTRUCTIONS

Loosely CO 50 sts.
Work in St st until 33".
BO and weave in ends.
Rep to make another rectangle.

ASSEMBLY

1. Measure 14" along the long side of one of the rectangles and pin one end of the other rectangle to the 14" section of the first rectangle, as in Figure 3-1.
2. Stitch together.
3. Repeat, measuring along the side of the second rectangle and sewing the end of the first rectangle along the 14" section.
4. Slip stitch along the neck opening to stabilize the edge.
5. Weave in ends.

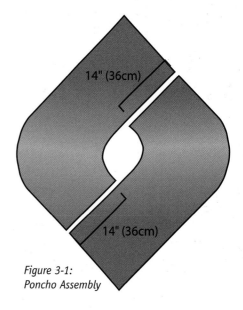

Figure 3-1:
Poncho Assembly

Elegant Slanting Stripes

EASY

The simplest of knit-purl patterns pairs perfectly with this elegant hand-dyed silk/wool blend yarn to create a classy accessory. Make it short like the one shown or keep going to make it as long as you choose.

Finished Size
7" x 36"
Gauge
(Measure in pattern stitch.)
17 sts and 20 rows = 4"

MATERIALS

· 1 skein (205yd/189m) light worsted silk blend yarn*
· Size 8 (5mm) needle

*Used in this project: 1 skein Lorna's Laces' Lion and Lamb (50% silk/50% wool, 205yd/189m, 3.5oz/100g), color #43ns Sage.

INSTRUCTIONS

CO 30 sts.
Follow Figure 3-2 or the line-by-line
  instructions below.
Row 1: (P1, k5) rep 5 times.
Row 2: P.
Row 3: K1, (p1, k5) rep 4 times, p1, k4.
Row 4: P.
Row 5: K2, (p1, k5) rep 4 times, p1, k3.
Row 6: P.
Row 7: K3, (p1, k5) rep 4 times, p1, k2.
Row 8: P.
Row 9: K4, (p1, k5) rep 4 times, p1, k1.
Row 10: P.
Row 11: (K5, p1) rep 5 times.
Row 12: P.
Rep rows 1 through 12 until 36" or desired length.
BO and weave in ends.

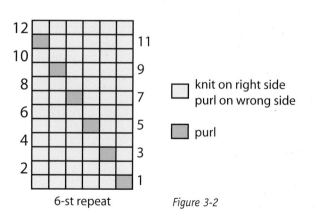

knit on right side
purl on wrong side

purl

6-st repeat

Figure 3-2

Simple Ascot

EASY

This texture-filled pattern is the work of a garter stitch, knit-purl rib concoction that's a cinch to memorize so you can knit it on the go with ease. Make it long or short, wide or narrow. Experiment with it by working a few more rows in garter stitch or the knit-purl rib and see what happens. It's a great jumping-off point for experimenting with texture in knit and purl stitches.

Finished Size
5" x 34"
Gauge
(Measure in pattern stitch.)
16 sts and 24 rows = 4"

MATERIALS
- 1 skein (190yd/175m) berry-color worsted-weight yarn*
- Size 9 (5.5mm) needles.

*Used in this project: 1 skein Brown Sheep's Lamb's Pride
(85% wool/15% mohair, 190yd/175m, 3.5oz/100g), color #M28 Chianti.

INSTRUCTIONS
CO 20 sts.
Follow Figure 3-3 or the line-by-line
  instructions below.
Row 1: (K1, p1) rep across.
Rows 2 and 3: K.
Rep rows 1 through 3 until 34" or desired length.
BO and weave in ends.

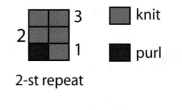

knit
purl

2-st repeat

Figure 3-3

Fanned Rib Scarf

INTERMEDIATE

This more intricate knit-purl pattern incorporates increases and decreases to make the ribbing pull in at the top and to create the center triangle pattern. All the increases are made by knitting into the front and the back of the stitch. So even though the design looks centered, the pattern is actually off by one stitch on the left, so the texture will be centered.

Finished Size
5" x 54"
Gauge
(Measure in stockinette stitch.)
16 sts and 22 rows = 4"

MATERIALS

· 2 balls (90yd/82m) Aran-style yarn*
· Size 9 (5.5mm) needles
· Stitch holder

*Used in this project: 2 balls Jaeger Yarn's Matchmaker Merino Aran (100% merino wool, 90yd/82m, 1.75oz/50g), color #770 Ice.

INSTRUCTIONS

CO 38 sts.
Rows 1 - 3: K.
Row 4: (P2, k2) rep 9 times, p2.
Row 5: (K2, p2) rep 9 times, k2.
Rows 6 - 13: Rep (rows 4 and 5) 4 times.
Row 14: P2, p2tog rep to last 2 sts, p2 - 21 sts.
Now, follow Figure 3-4 or continue with the line-by-line instructions below.
Row 15: K1, p1, inc, k6, s2kp, k5, inc, k1, p1, k1.
Row 16: P1, k1, p17, k1, p1.
Row 17: P1, k1, p1, inc, k5, s2kp, k4, inc, (k1, p1) twice.
Row 18: K1, p1, k1, p15, k1, p1, k1.
Row 19: (K1, p1) twice, inc, k4, s2kp, k3, inc, (k1, p1) twice, k1.
Row 20: K2, p1, k1, p13, k1, p1, k2.
Row 21: K2, p1, k1, p1, inc, k3, s2kp, k2, inc, (k1, p1) twice, k2.
Row 22: K3, p1, k1, p11, k1, p1, k3.
Row 23: K3, p1, k1, p1, inc, k2, s2kp, k1, inc, (k1, p1) twice, k3.
Row 24: K4, p1, k1, p9, k1, p1, k4.
Row 25: K4, p1, k1, p1, inc, k1, s2kp, inc, (k1, p1) twice, k4.
Row 26: K3, (p1, k1) twice, p7, (k1, p1) twice, k3.
Row 27: K5, p1, k1, p1, inc, s2kp, M1, (k1, p1) twice, k5.
Row 28: K3, p2, k1, p1, k1,p5, k1, p1, k1, p2, k3.
Row 29: K6, p1, k1, p1, k3, p1, k1, p1, k6.
Row 30: K3, p3, k1, p1, k1, p3, k1, p1, k1, p3, k3.

Row 31: K7, (p1, k1) rep 4 times, k6.
Row 32: K3, p4, (k1, p1) rep 4 times, p3, k3.
Row 33: K8, (p1, k1) rep 3 times, k7.
Row 34: K3, p5, (k1, p1) rep 3 times, p4, k3.
Row 35: K9, p1, k1, p1, k9.
Row 36: K3, p6, k1, p1, k1, p6, k3.
Row 37: K10, p1, k10.
Row 38: K3, p7, k1, p7, k3.
Row 39: K.
Row 40: K3, p15, k3.
Rep rows 39 and 40 until 27" from beg of patt.
Move to a stitch holder and follow the instructions again for the other half of the scarf, stopping one fewer row than the first half.
Graft 2 halves tog.

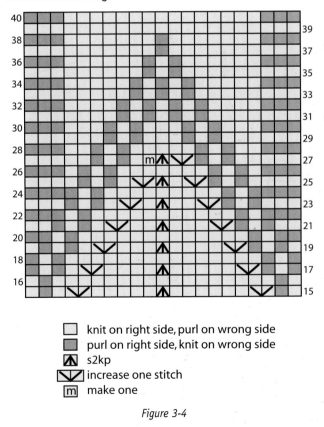

knit on right side, purl on wrong side
purl on right side, knit on wrong side
s2kp
increase one stitch
m make one

Figure 3-4

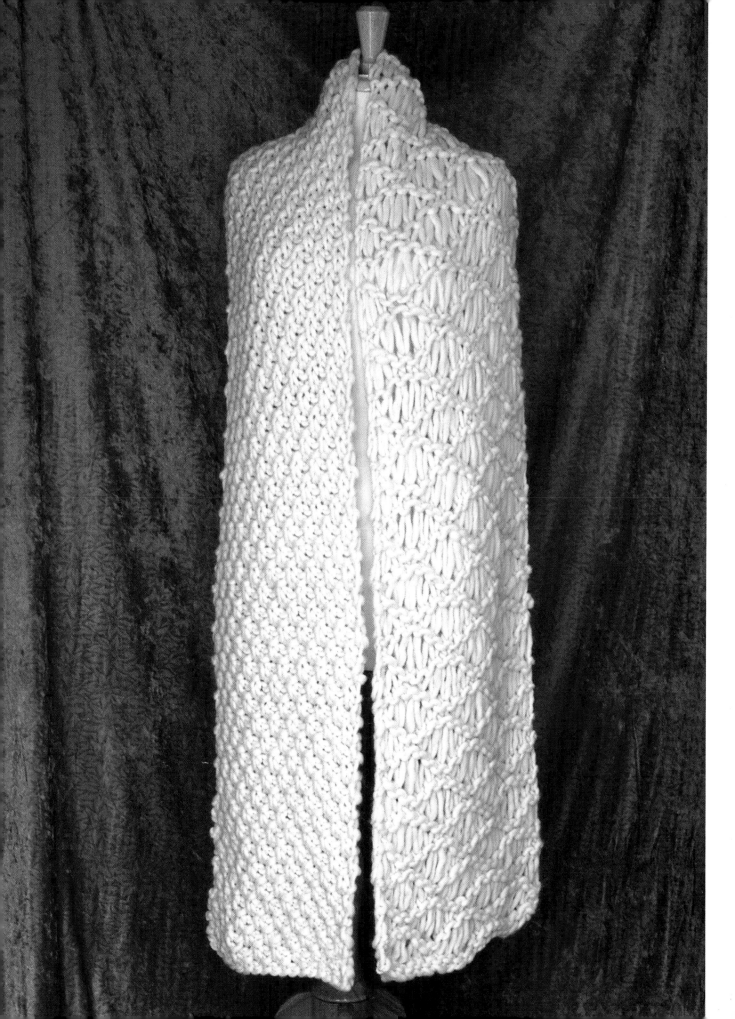

Winter White Two-Pattern Scarf

This huge warm-and-wooly scarf is as soft and cozy as it is full of texture. One side is worked in classic moss stitch, which is a simple knit-purl repeat, while the other side is a diamond pattern that's often used to show off variegated yarns. But here in white, both patterns look beautiful and the thick wool roving is oh-so-soft!

EASY

Finished Size
10" to 12" x 96"
Gauge
(Measure first 4 rows of moss stitch.)
7 sts and 8 rows = 4"

MATERIALS

- 2 skeins (123yd/113m) natural white super bulky roving*
- Size 35 (19mm) needles

*Used in this project: Cascade Yarns' Magnum (100% pure new wool, 123yd/113m, 8.82oz/250g), color #0010.

INSTRUCTIONS

CO 19 sts.
Follow Figures 3-5 and 3-6 or the line-by-line instructions that follow.

Moss st patt:

- Row 1: (K1, p1) rep to last st, k1.
- Row 2: (P1, k1) rep to last st, p1.
- Row 3: (P1, k1) rep to last st, p1.
- Row 4: (K1, p1) rep to last st, k1.
- Repeat rows 1 through 4 until you have almost finished 1 skein of yarn. On the last rep, change to the new skein of yarn by spreading the yarn ends apart, overlapping them and k them tog as you work the row.

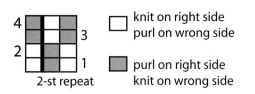

Figure 3-5: Moss Stitch Pattern

Dropped st diamond patt:

- Row 1: (K2, yo, k1, yo twice, k1, yo twice, k1, yo, k1) rep 3 times, k1.
- Row 2: K1, (k1, drp1, k1, drp2, k1, drp2, k1, drp1, k2) rep 3 times.
- Row 3: (K1, yo twice, k1, yo, k3, yo, k1, yo twice) rep 3 times, k1.
- Row 4: K1, (drp2, k1, drp1, k3, drp1, k1, drp2, k1) rep 3 times.
- Rep rows 1 through 4 until 96" from beg moss st patt.

BO and weave in ends.

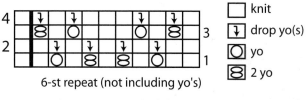

6-st repeat (not including yo's)

Figure 3-6: Dropped-Stitch Diamond Pattern

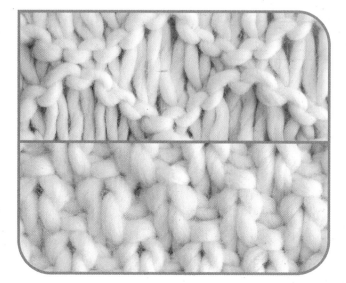

PONCHO VARIATION

You will need the same amount of yarn
 as for the scarf.

CO 27 sts.

Follow Figure 3-5 on the previous page or the
 line-by-line instructions below.

Moss st patt:
- Row 1: (K1, p1) rep to last st, k1.
- Row 2: (K1, k1) rep to last st, p1.
- Row 3: (K1, k1) rep to last st, p1.
- Row 4: (K1, p1) rep to last st, k1.
- Rep rows 1 through 4 until 33".

BO and weave in ends.

Rep moss st patt to make another rectangle.

Assemble as in the Easy Evening Poncho on
 page 53.

Cables

Cables are a classic knitting technique that can range from simple, small patterns to intricately detailed designs full of left and right crossings that boggle the mind. Cables are also great for making pictorial images in knitwear. Here are three designs that range from basic to more complex, with a little knit-purl texture added for an Aran feel. The first pattern has the cable instructions written out so it is easier to follow, while the other two patterns use the (#)lx(#) and (#)rx(#) abbreviations, although the Gray Rustic Celtic uses a variation.

Classic Cable Scarf

EASY

MEDIUM
4
MOYEN
Medio

This easy cable scarf presents a standard design that is classic and straightforward. It's a great introduction to cable knitting. By using a wonderful yarn, like this beautiful hand-dyed pink yarn with the color variations meandering through the piece, you add interest and movement to enhance a very basic design.

Finished Size
6" x 45"
Gauge
(Measure in cable pattern stitch.)
21 sts and 19 rows = 4"

MATERIALS

· 1 skein (190yd/175m) worsted-weight yarn*
· Size 10½ (6.5mm) knitting needles
· Cable needle

*Used in this project: 1 skein Lorna's Laces' Bullfrogs and Butterflies (85% wool/15% mohair, 190yd/175m), color #23ns Berry.

INSTRUCTIONS

CO 32 sts.
Follow Figure 4-1 or the line-by-line
  instructions below.
Row 1: (K2, p2, k4, p2) 3 times, k2.
Row 2: (P2, k2, p4, k2) 3 times, p2.
Rows 3 - 8: Rep rows 1 and 2.
Row 9: (K2, p2, 2 sts to cable needle in front, k2,
  k2 from cable needle, p2) 3 times, k2.
Row 10: Rep row 2.
Rep rows 3 through 10 26 times or until
  desired length.
Rep (rows 1 and 2) 3 times.
BO in patt.

10 - st repeat

▨ knit on right side, purl on wrong side

■ purl on wrong side, knit on right side

▨ two over two, left cross

Figure 4-1

Aran-Style Scarf

INTERMEDIATE

LIGHT
3
LEGER
Ligero

Aran knitting is characterized by a highly textured surface, usually with small, textured patterns on the sides and a center pattern that is larger. The patterns are often separated by vertical lines of knit-purl ribs or small cables. With or without cables, Aran patterns definitely have lots of knit-purl texture like the moss stitch on the sides of this scarf.

Finished Size
7" x 56"
Gauge
(Measure in pattern stitch.)
18 sts and 21 rows = 4"

MATERIALS

- 2 skeins (200yd/185m) light worsted-weight yarn*
- Size 9 (5.5mm) needles
- Cable needle

*Used in this project: Harrisville Designs' New England Knitter's Highland (100% pure virgin wool, 200yd/185m, 3.5oz/100g), color #13 Peacock.

INSTRUCTIONS

CO 32 sts.
Follow Figure 4-2 or the following line-by-line instructions.
Row 1: (P1, k1) twice, p1, k1, p1, k2, p1, k1, p1, k8, p1, k1, p1, k2, p1, k1, p1, (k1, p1) twice.
Row 2 and all WS rows: P the k sts and k the p sts.
Row 3: (K1, p1) twice, p1, k1, p1, k2, p1, k1, p1, k8, p1, k1, p1, k2, p1, k1, p1, (p1, k1) twice.
Row 5: (P1, k1) twice, p1, k1, p1, 1rx1, p1, k1, p1, 2lx2, 2rx2, p1, k1, p1, 1rx1, p1, k1, p1, (k1, p1) twice.
Rep rows 2 through 5 until 56" from beg of patt or until desired length.
Work 2 more rows in patt.
BO and weave in ends.

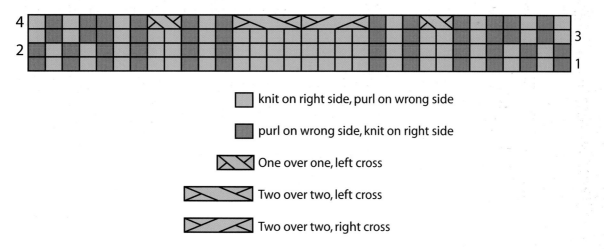

| knit on right side, purl on wrong side |
| purl on wrong side, knit on right side |
| One over one, left cross |
| Two over two, left cross |
| Two over two, right cross |

Figure 4-2

Gray Rustic Celtic

This intricate-looking cable pattern is easier to accomplish than it appears. Working on large needles with two strands of yarn held together as one makes the knitting go fast, and the actual pattern is knit two-purl two with garter stitch edges. You only have to concentrate on the rows where you twist the cables, as the rest of the rows are all easy knitting!

Finished Size
10" x 64"
Gauge
(Measure in pattern stitch.)
16 sts and 13 rows = 4"

MATERIALS
- 2 skeins (525yd/485m) light worsted-weight yarn*
- Size 13 (9mm) needles
- Cable needles

*Used in this project: 2 skeins Baabajoe's 8-ply Woolpaks (100% pure New Zealand wool, 525 yd/485m, 9oz/250g), color Tussock.

INSTRUCTIONS
Hold 2 strands yarn tog as 1 throughout.
Because you are making the cable over the purl rib, the cable crossing is a little more complex than a basic right or left cross. Here is how to make the left (2lx4) and right (2rx4) cross steps:

- For 2lx4: 2 sts to cable needles in front, 2 sts to cable needles in back, k2, p2 from cable needles in back, k2 from cable needles in front.
- For 2rx4: 4 sts to cable needles in back, k2, move 2 p sts to LH needle, move rem sts on cable needles to front, p 2 sts on left needle, k sts from cable needles.

CO 40 sts.
Follow Figure 4-3 on the next page or the line-by-line instructions below.
Row 1: K3, (p2, k2) rep 8 times, p2, k3.
Row 2: K5, (p2, k2) rep 8 times, k3.
Row 3 - 6: Rep rows 1 and 2.
Row 7: K3, p2, k2, p2, 2lx4, (p2, k2) twice, p2, 2lx4, p2, k2, p2, k3.
Row 8 and all even rows: Rep row 2.
Row 9: Rep row 1.
Row 11: K3, (p2, 2rx4) rep 4 times, p2, k3.
Row 13: Rep row 1.
Row 15: K3, p2, k2 (p2, 2lx4) rep 3 times, p2, k2, p2, k3.
Row 17: Rep row 1.
Row 19: K3, (p2, k2) rep 3 times, p2, 2lx4, (p2, k2) rep 3 times, p2, k3.
Row 21: Rep row 1.
Row 23: Rep row 15.
Row 25: Rep row 1.
Row 27: Rep row 11.
Row 29: Rep row 1.
Row 31: Rep row 7.
Rows 33 and 35: Rep row 1.
Row 37: Rep row 19.
Row 39: Rep row 1.
Row 40: Rep row 2.
Rep (rows 3 through 40) 4 more times.
Rep rows 3 through 36.
BO and weave in ends.

work rows 1 through 6
repeat rows 7 through 42 six times
repeat rows 7 thorugh 36
repeat row 1 and row 2
BO

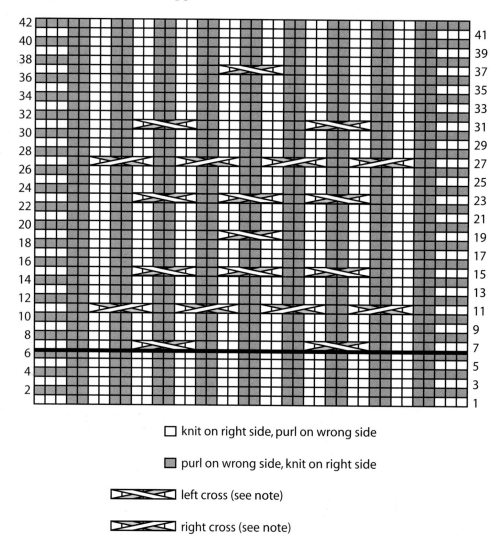

☐ knit on right side, purl on wrong side

▨ purl on wrong side, knit on right side

left cross (see note)

right cross (see note)

Figure 4-3

Chapter 5

Lace

It truly is amazing how a little yarn-over (probably someone's mistake way back when) can transform your knitting into fabulous lacework! These projects cover a range of lace, from a narrow six-stitch pattern to a long lace shawl. All explore the fun that can be had with lace knitting.

Apple Green Roving Scarf

EASY

I don't think most people would consider this scarf to be lace, but the yarn-overs and knitting-togethers are enough like lace to me to place it in this category. It's a great way to try out the technique and see if you like it, while whipping up the fastest scarf in town! The beautiful green color of the hand-dyed roving is wonderful to work with, too. Just six stitches, huge needles and yarn are a great introduction to openwork knitting and lace.

Finished Size
3½" x 54"
Gauge
(Measure in pattern stitch.)
7 sts and 7 rows = 4"

MATERIALS

· 1 skein (45yd/42m) green super bulky roving yarn*
· Size 35 (19mm) needles

*Used in this project: 1 skein Blue Sky Alpacas' Bulky Hand Dyes (50% alpaca/50% wool, 45yd/42m, 3.5oz/100g), color #1011 Granny Smith.

INSTRUCTIONS

CO 1 st.
Follow Figure 5-1 or the line-by-line instructions below.
Row 1: Inc 1 - 2 sts.
Row 2: Inc 1 twice - 4 sts.
Row 3: K1, yo, k2, yo, k1 - 6 sts.
Row 4: K2 (yo, k2tog) twice.
Rep row 4 until 52" from beg of patt or 2" less than desired length.
Dec rows as follows:
  • Row 1: (K2tog, yo) twice, k2tog - 5 sts.
  • Row 2: K2tog, k1, k2tog - 3 sts.
  • Row 3: K3tog - 1 st.
Cut yarn, pass through rem st and weave in end.

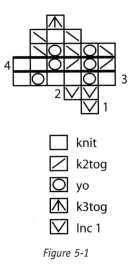

	knit
⊘	k2tog
◯	yo
⩘	k3tog
⋁	Inc 1

Figure 5-1

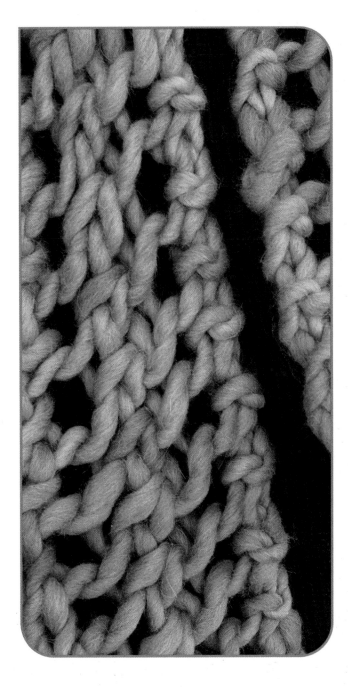

White Lace Scarf

EASY

LIGHT
3
LEGER
Ligero

The wonderful airy feel of this little lace scarf is what makes it so special. The simple pattern repeat is easy to memorize so that you can work on this one anywhere while your fingers deftly create a little bit of charm.

Finished Size
3¾" x 60"
Gauge
(Measure in lace pattern.)
17 sts and rows = 4"

Designed by Lois Varga

MATERIALS
· 2 skeins (93yd/85m) DK weight cotton blend yarn*
· Size 7 (4.5mm) needles
· Stitch marker

*Used in this project: 2 skeins Classic Elite Yarns' Imagine (53% cotton/47% rayon, 93yd/85m, 1.75oz/50g), color #9201 White.

INSTRUCTIONS
CO 16 sts.
Row 1: K1, p1, k14, p1, k1.

Row 2: K1, p1, (k into 2nd st on LH needle, k into 1st st on LH needle, sl both sts to RH needle) rep to last 2 sts, p1, k1.

Row 3: K1, p1, k1, (k into 2nd st on LH needle, k into 1st st on LH needle, sl both sts to RH needle) rep to last 3 sts, k1, p1, k1.

Row 4: Rep row 2.

Row 5: K1, p1, (yo, k2tog) repeat to last 2 sts, p1, k1.

Row 6: K1, p1, k14, p1, k1.

Rep rows 2 through 6 until 60" from beg of patt.

BO and weave in ends.

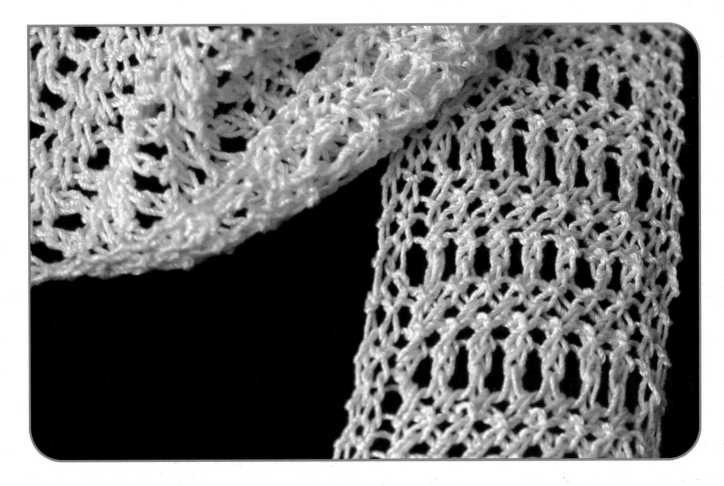

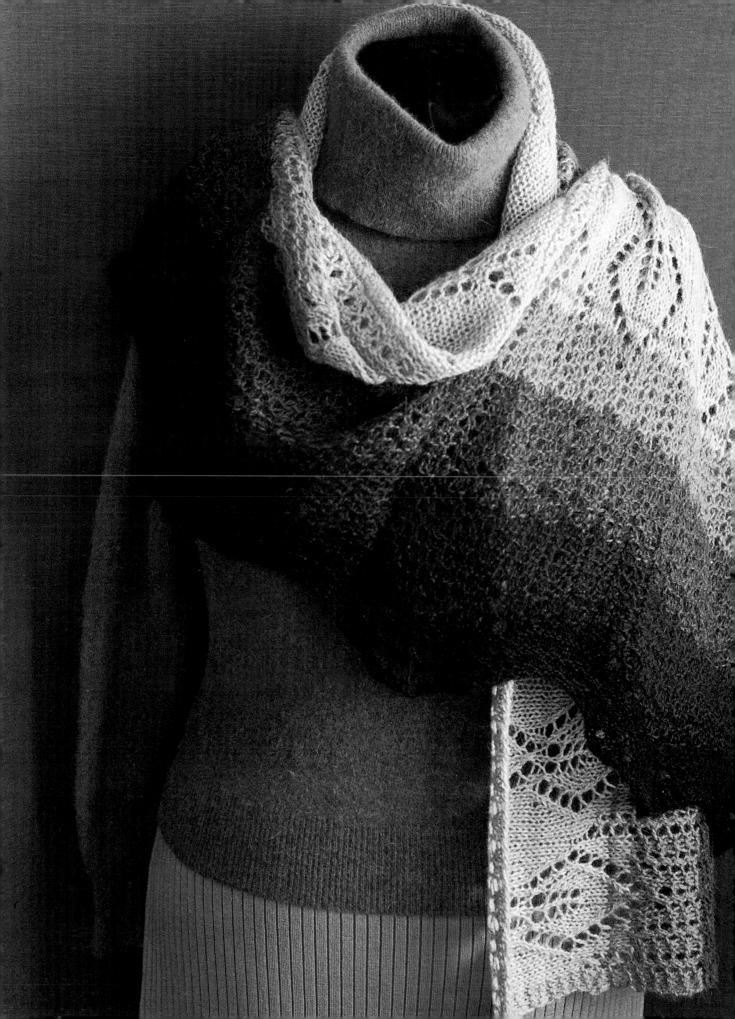

Lacy Leaves Shawl

Make this lacy pattern as wide or as long as you want. You could make it as instructed, or only make two repeats of the design and knit the repeated openwork row until you have a long, long scarf with one end a leaf and the other a black scallop. There are many ways to use these designs.

EXPERIENCED

FINE
2
FIN
Fino

Finished Size
66" x 18"
Gauge
(Measure in garter stitch.)
18 sts and 22 rows = 4"

MATERIALS

· 6 balls (134yd/124m) sport-weight yarn in six light to dark colors*
· Size 7 (4.5mm) needles

*Used in this project: 1 ball each Blue Sky Alpacas' 100% Alpaca (100% alpaca, 134yd/124m, 2oz/56g), colors #005 Taupe, #004 Light Tan, #003 Medium Tan, #008 Streaky Brown, #001 Dark Brown and #100 Black.

INSTRUCTIONS

CO 280 sts in lightest colored yarn.

Follow lace patt A and B on Figure 5-2 through row 39, changing yarn colors as shown in the chart. (Work from from lightest to the next darker color for each color change.)

Rep lace patt C once in third-lightest color yarn, then 7 times in next color and 6 times in the next color.

Alternate 2 more rep of patt C with the darkest color and the second-to-darkest color.

Work patt D twice in the darkest color.

BO very loosely on wrong side in St st and weave in ends.

Wet in warm water, press out excess water and block to size. Let dry.

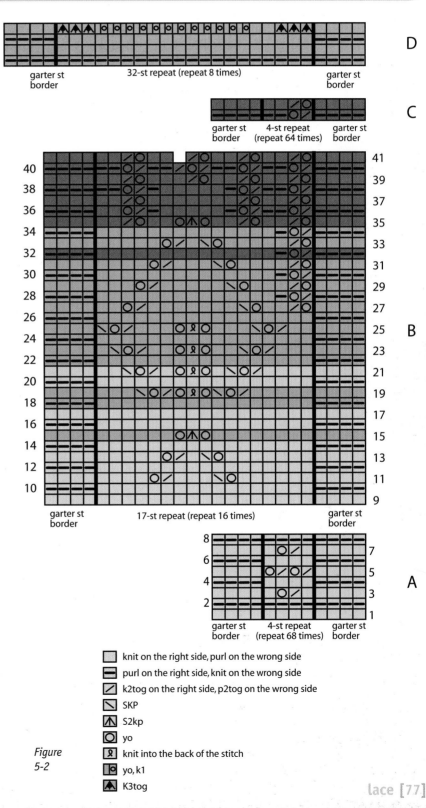

Figure 5-2

knit on the right side, purl on the wrong side
purl on the right side, knit on the wrong side
k2tog on the right side, p2tog on the wrong side
SKP
S2kp
yo
knit into the back of the stitch
yo, k1
K3tog

Winter Mountains Scarf

A flowing river with mountains in the background, and the snow is falling…these are the images I thought of as I was working on this pattern. The soft blue yarn is like the blue in ice or in a light blue sky and the fringe is like a waterfall flowing out of the river.

Finished Size
8" x 60", not including 4" fringe
Gauge
(Measure in stockinette stitch.)
19½ sts and 24 rows = 4"

MATERIALS

- 3 balls (131yd/120m) light blue DK weight yarn*
- Size 7 needles
- Stitch holder
- Size H crochet hook

*Used in this project: 3 balls Jaeger's Baby Merino DK (100% merino wool, 131yd/120m, 1.75oz/50g), color #222 Powder.

INSTRUCTIONS

CO 36 sts.
Follow Figure 5-3 or the following line-by-line instructions.
Row 1: K1, k2tog, yo, k2, (yo, k1) rep 5 times, k2tog 4 times, k3tog, k2tog 4 times, k1 (k1, yo) rep 5 times, k2, yo, skp, k1.
Row 2 and all WS rows: P.
Row 3: K.
Row 5: Rep row 1.
Rows 6 - 8: Rep rows 2 through 5.
Rows 9 - 10: Work in St st.
Row 11: K2, k2tog, yo, k6, yo, skp, k2, (yo, skp) twice, yo, k3tog, (yo, k2tog) twice, yo, k2, k2tog, yo, k6, yo, k2tog, k2.

Row 13: K11, yo, skp, k2, (yo, skp) twice, k1, (k2tog, yo) twice, k2, k2tog, yo, k11.
Row 15: K2tog, yo, k2, k2tog, yo, k6, yo, skp, k2, yo, skp, yo, k3tog, yo, k2tog, yo, k2, k2tog, yo, k6, yo, skp, k2, yo, skp.
Row 17: K2, k2tog, yo, k2, yo, skp, k3, k2tog, yo, skp, k2, yo, skp, k1, k2tog, yo, k2, k2tog, yo, k6, yo, skp, k2, yo, skp.
Row 19: K6, k2tog, yo, (k4, k2tog, yo) rep 5 times, k7.
Row 21: K1, k2tog, yo, k to last 3 sts, yo, skp, k1.
Row 23: K1, k2tog, yo, k2, (k4, k2tog, yo) rep 4 times, k7, yo, skp, k1.
Row 25: Rep row 21.
Row 27: Rep row 19.
Row 29: Rep row 21.
Work in St st until 30" from beg of patt.
Move to stitch holder.
Rep instructions for the other scarf half.
Graft tog 2 halves.

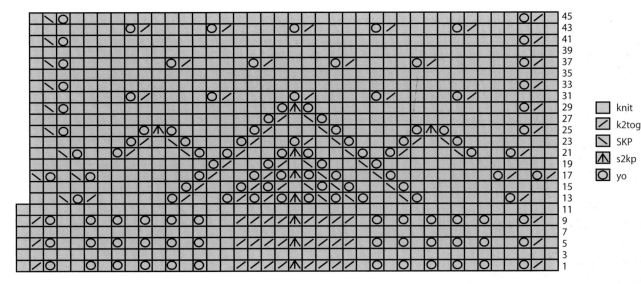

☐	knit
╱	k2tog
╲	SKP
⋀	s2kp
O	yo

Figure 5-3

FRINGE

1. Cut 100 8½" lengths of yarn.
2. Fold in half in pairs of two.

3. Use the crochet hook to attach each pair along the edge of the scarf, attaching the strands so they are right next to each other and using more or fewer pairs as needed to cover the edge of the scarf.

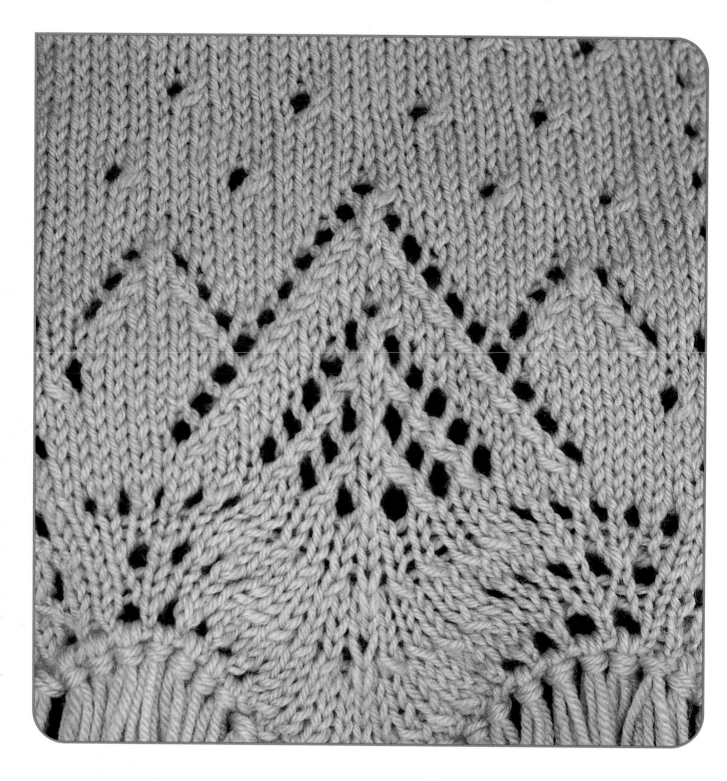

Chapter 6

Beads

Knitting with beads is a technique that can greatly enhance the ends of a scarf. With just a little practice, you can add a whole new texture to your knitting. From simple bead stripes to more intricate knit and purl patterns, you have many possibilities for added texture and color when adding beads to your knitting. If you are new to knitting with beads, be sure to read the Basics section covering how to string beads and how to work with them in knitting, page 26.

Easy Beaded Scarf

INTERMEDIATE

FINE
2
FIN
Fino

This is the scarf I demonstrated on Creative Living *with Sheryl Borden several years ago. It is easy and fun to do because you are simply knitting each row and sliding beads between stitches to make the pattern.*

Finished Size 7½" x 46"
Gauge
(Measure in garter stitch.)
24 sts and 22 rows = 4"

MATERIALS

- 4 skeins (126yd/115m) sport-weight yarn the beads fit onto*
- 52 grams or 2,160 size 8 purple-lined seed beads
- Size 3 (3.25mm) needles
- Stitch holder
- Size 11 beading needle and waste thread to string the beads

* Used in this project: Dale of Norway's Tiur (60% mohair/40% pure new wool, 126yd/115m, 1.75oz/50g), color #5172 Purple.

INSTRUCTIONS

String 1,080 beads (half) onto one ball of yarn.
CO row: (45) Using a simple CO, CO 3 sts, slide 5 beads up to needle, (CO 2 sts, slide 5 beads up to needle) 8 times, CO 3 sts (22 sts and 9 groups of 5 beads).

Rows 1 - 7: (45) K3, b5, (k2, b5) 8 times, k3.
Row 8: (36) K3, b4 (k1, inc 1, k1, b4) 8 times, k3 (30 sts).
Rows 9 - 15: (36) K3, b4, (k3, b4) 8 times, k3.
Row 16: (27) K3, b3 (k2, inc 1, k1, B3) 8 times, k3 (38 sts).
Rows 17 - 23: (27) K3, b3, (k4, b3) 8 times, k3.
Row 24: (18) K3, b2 (k2, inc 1, k2, b2) 8 times, k3 (46 sts).
Rows 25 - 31: (18) K3, b2, (k5, b2) 8 times, k3.
Rows 32 - 39: (9) K3, b1, (k5, b1) 8 times, k3.
Work in garter st until 23" from beg of patt.
Move to stitch holder.
Rep instructions for the other end of scarf.
Graft pieces tog in the middle.
Weave in ends.

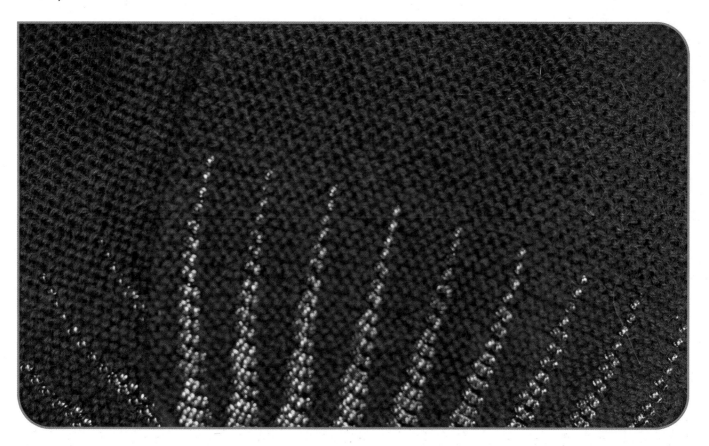

Lavender Scarf

INTERMEDIATE

FINE
2
FIN
FINO
Fino

This luxurious little scarf is made from a soft, silky alpaca blend that complements the beads quite nicely. The tapering diamond shape of the bead pattern adds elegance to the design. It's an easy pattern to work, too!

Finished Size
4¾" x 44"

MATERIALS

- 2 skeins (123yd/114m) amethyst sport-weight yarn that beads fit onto*
- 286 size 8 seed beads
- Size 4 (3.5mm) needles
- Stitch holder
- Size 11 beading needle and thread

*Used in this project: 2 skeins of Cascade Yarns' Indulgence (70% Superfine alpaca/30% angora, 123yd/114m, 50g/1.75oz) color #521 Amethyst.

INSTRUCTIONS

String 143 beads (half) onto 1 yarn ball.
CO 4 sts.
Row 1 and all odd-numbered rows: p.
Follow Figure 6-1 on the next page or
  the line-by-line instructions below.
Row 2: K1, yo, k2, yo, k1 - 6 sts.
Row 4: (1) K1, yo, k1, p1, b1, p1, k1, yo, k1 - 8 sts.
Row 6: (2) K1, yo, k1, p1, b1, p2, b1, p1, k1, yo, k1 - 10 sts.
Row 8: (3) K1, yo, k1, p1, b1, p2, b1, p2, b1, p1, k1, yo, k1 - 12 sts.
Row 10: (4) K1, yo, k1, p1, b1, p2, b1, p2, b1, p2, b1, p1, k1, yo, k1 - 14 sts.
Row 12: (5) K1, yo, k1, p1, b1, p2, b1, p2, b1, p2, b1, p2, b1, p1, k1, yo, k1 - 16 sts.
Row 14: (6) K1, yo, k1, p1, b1, p2, b1, p2, b1, p2, b1, p2, b1, p2, b1, p1, k1, yo, k1 - 18 sts.
Row 16: (7) K1, yo, k1, p1, b1, p2, b1, p2, b1, p2, b1, p2, b1, p2, b1, p2, b1, p1, k1, yo, k1 - 20 sts.
Row 18: (8) K1, yo, k1, p1, b1, p2, b1, p2, b1, p2, b1, p2, b1, p2, b1, p2, b1, p2, b1, p1, k1, yo, k1 - 22 sts.
Row 20: (9) K1, yo, k1, p1, b1, p2, b1, p2, b1, p2, b1, p2, b1, p2, b1, p2, b1, p2, b1, p2, b1, p1, k1, yo, k1 - 24 sts.
Row 22: (10) K1, yo, k1, p1, b1, p2, b1, p2, b1, p2, b1, p2, b1, p2, b1, p2, b1, p2, b1, p2, b1, p2, b1, p1, k1, yo, k1 - 26 sts.
Row 24: (11) K1, yo, k1, p1, b1, p2, b1, p2, b1, p2, b1, p2, b1, p2, b1, p2, b1, p2, b1, p2, b1, p2, b1, p2, b1, p1, k1, yo, k1 - 28 sts.
Row 26: (12) K1, yo, k1, p1, b1, p2, b1, p2, b1, p2, b1, p2, b1, p2, b1, p2, b1, p2, b1, p2, b1, p2, b1, p2, b1, p2, b1, p1, k1, yo, k1 - 30 sts.
Row 28: (9) K1, yo, k2tog, k3, p1, b1, p2, b1, p2, b1, p2, b1, p2, b1, p2, b1, p2, b1, p2, b1, p2, b1, p1, k3, skp, yo, k1.
Row 30: (8) K1, yo, k2tog, k4, p1, b1, p2, b1, p2, b1, p2, b1, p2, b1, p2, b1, p2, b1, p2, b1, p1, k4, skp, yo, k1.

Row 32: (7) K1, yo, k2tog, k5, p1, b1, p2, b1, p2, b1, p2, b1, p2, b1, p2, b1, p1, k5, skp, yo, k1.

Row 34: (6) K1, yo, k2tog, k6, p1, b1, p2, b1, p2, b1, p2, b1, p2, b1, p2, b1, p1, k6, skp, yo, k1.

Row 36: (5) K1, yo, k2tog, k7, p1, b1, p2, b1, p2, b1, p2, b1, p2, b1, p1, k7, skp, yo, k1.

Row 38: (4) K1, yo, k2tog, k8, p1, b1, p2, b1, p2, b1, p2, b1, p1, k8, skp, yo, k1.

Row 40: (5) K1, yo, k2tog, k7, p1, b1, p2, b1, p2, b1, p2, b1, p2, b1, p1, k7, skp, yo, k1.

Row 42: (4) K1, yo, k2tog, k8, p1, b1, p2, b1, p2, b1, p2, b1, p1, k8, skp, yo, k1.

Row 44: (3) K1, yo, k2tog, k9, p1, b1, p2, b1, p2, b1, p1, k9, skp, yo, k1.

Row 46: (2) K1, yo, k2tog, k10, p1, b1, p2, b1, p1, k10, skp, yo, k1.

Row 48: (3) K1, yo, k2tog, k9, p1, b1, p2, b1, p2, b1, p1, k9, skp, yo, k1.

Row 50: (2) K1, yo, k2tog, k10, p1, b1, p2, b1, p1, k10, skp, yo, k1.

Row 52: (1) K1, yo, k2tog, k11, p1, b1, p1, k11, skp, yo, k1.

Row 54: (2) K1, yo, k2tog, k10, p1, b1, p2, b1, p1, k10, skp, yo, k1.

Row 56: (1) K1, yo, k2tog, k11, p1, b1, p1, k11, skp, yo, k1.

Row 58: (1) K1, yo, k2tog, k11, p1, b1, p1, k11, skp, yo, k1.

Row 60: (1) K1, yo, k2tog, k11, p1, b1, p1, k11, skp, yo, k1.

Row 62: (1) K1, yo, k2tog, k11, p1, b1, p1, k11, skp, yo, k1.

Rows 64 – 118: K1, yo, k2tog, k24, skp, yo, k1.
Move knitting to the stitch holder.
String rem 143 beads onto other yarn ball.
Rep instructions for other scarf half.
Graft pieces tog in the middle.

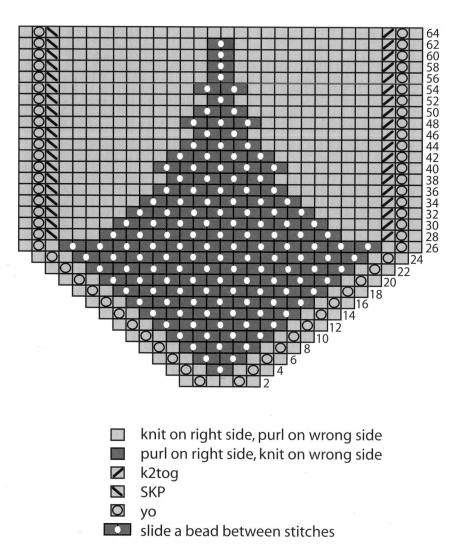

knit on right side, purl on wrong side

purl on right side, knit on wrong side

k2tog

SKP

yo

slide a bead between stitches

Figure 6-1

Chapter 7

Embroidery

Scarves and shawls are a great surface for experimenting with embroidery, especially if you felt your knitting first as in the Felted Old-Time Embroidered Scarf, page 90. Beads and pulled-thread embroidery are also great venues for fun.

Simple Pulled-Thread Scarf

EASY

LIGHT
3
LEGER
Ligero

Here's a new thing to do with knitting: pulled-thread embroidery. Because the knitting is pliable, it can be pulled, just as in pulled-thread embroidery, creating openwork designs that add the texture.

Finished Size
6" x 70"
Gauge
20 sts and 26 rows = 4"

MATERIALS
· 3 balls (130yd/120m) yellow-green DK weight yarn*
· Size 6 (4mm) needles
· Tapestry needle

*Used in this project: 3 balls Jaeger's Matchmaker Merino DK (100% merino wool, 130yd/120m, 1.75oz/50g), color #886 Asparagus.

INSTRUCTIONS
CO 30 sts.
Work in St st until 70" from beg of patt.
BO and weave in ends.

EMBROIDERY

1. Stitch across the fifth row from each end of the scarf, with the scarf end away from you. Take the horizontal stitches around two knitted stitches and the slanting stitches over two knitted stitches and two rows of knitting, following the steps shown in Figure 7-1.

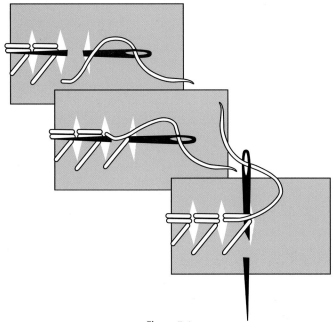

Figure 7-1

2. Finish the sides in buttonhole stitch, beginning a half-row in from the edge and spacing each stitch over two rows and two stitches of knitting, following the step shown in Figure 7-2.

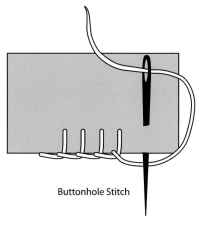

Buttonhole Stitch

Figure 7-2

3. Weave in ends.

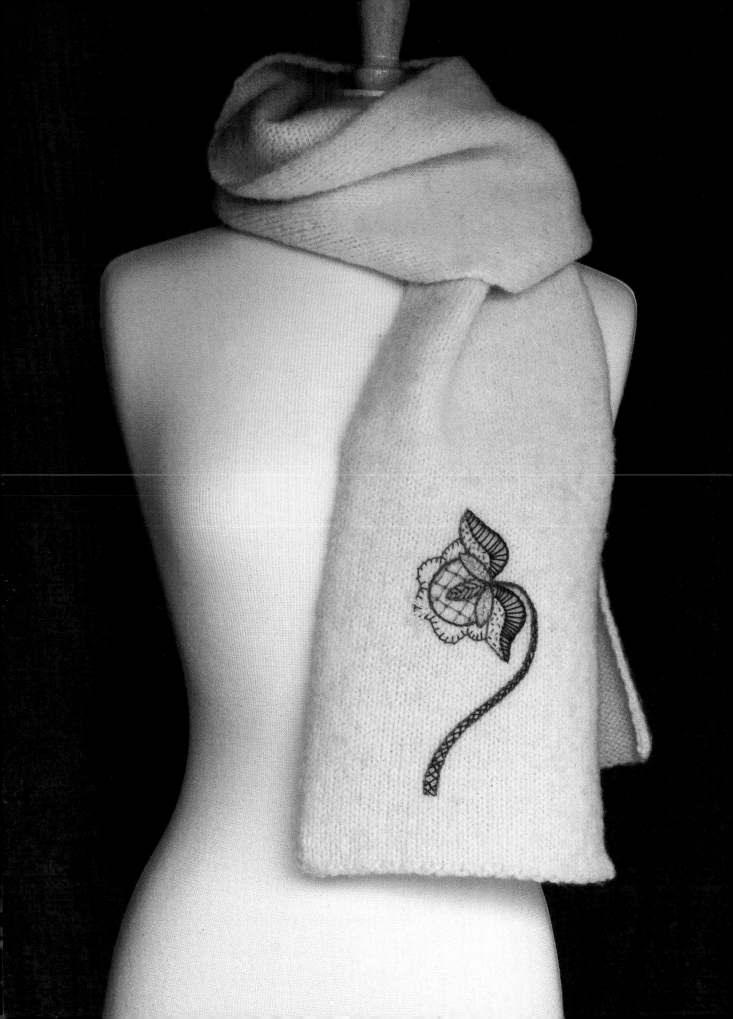

Felted Old-Time Flower-Embroidered Scarf

This quaint little design is easy to embroider on the felted surface of this scarf because the felting creates a nice dense area that keeps the embroidery stitching from sliding between any knitted stitches.

Finished Size
8" x 60" (depends on how much finished scarf is felted)
Gauge
(Measure in stockinette stitch.)
16 sts and 23 rows = 4"

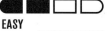

EASY

MEDIUM
4
MOYEN
Medio

MATERIALS

- 1 skein (465yd/425m) worsted-weight yarn*
- Size 9 (5.5mm) needles
- 1 ball size 10 crochet cotton
- Tapestry needle
- Embroidery needle
- Single-strand embroidery thread*, as follows:
  - 1 skein light sage green
  - 1 skein dark sage green
  - 1 skein light teal green
  - 1 skein dark teal green
  - 1 skein light coral
  - 1 skein dark Indian red
  - 1 skein golden yellow

*Used in this project: 1 skein Lion Brand Yarn's Fishermen's Wool (100% pure virgin wool, 465yd/425m, 8oz/227g), color #098 Natural and Impressions embroidery thread by Caron (50% silk, 50% wool, 36yd/33m), colors #5002 Light Sage Green, #5000 Dark Sage Green, #7024 Light Teal Green, #7022 Dark Teal Green, #2075 Coral, #178 Indian Red and #4003 Golden Yellow.

INSTRUCTIONS

CO 40 sts.
Work in St st until 70" from beg.
BO and weave in ends.

FELTING

1. Fold the scarf in half so it is 8" x 35".
2. Baste the scarf sides and ends together using the tapestry needle and crochet cotton.
3. Put scarf in the washing machine on hot/cold washer setting with 1 Tbsp. of liquid dish soap and the lowest water level setting.
4. Check the scarf halfway through the wash cycle to see if it is felted. If it is felting unevenly, pull it back to shape and return it to the washer. If it is completely felted, set the machine to the spin cycle and return the scarf to the washer. (See Tip on the next page.)

TIP: *Felting is a fascinating technique that transforms knitted wool into a dense, felted material. The transition can be stopped at any point in the process, creating a variety of degrees of feltedness. Slightly felted knitting is when you can still see the stitches, while fully felted knitting is when the stitches are completely indistinguishable and the fabric has a thick, soft, fuzzy surface. The degree to which you felt your project is often a choice of personal preference.*

For this scarf (step 4), the knitting should be felted enough that the stitches are locked together so you can embroider on the surface easily, but not so felted that the scarf is too thick and stiff to use.

It can be a tricky process if you want to make sure your piece is felted enough, but not too much. The best way I have found when felting items in the washing machine is to check on them often so that I can take them out as soon as they are felted to the degree I want.

5. Check it again at the end of the wash cycle, during the rinse cycle and at the end of the rinse cycle. If at any of these stages it is done felting, set the machine to the spin cycle to finish the felting process.
6. Remove the basting stitches and let the scarf dry hanging on a hanger in a warm place.

EMBROIDERY

1. Use embroidery thread and needle to stitch the flower design, as in Figure 7-3 on facing page and referring to the stitch illustrations below, if needed.
2. Stitch the filling stitches of the stem, leaves and flower first.
3. Stitch the outline stitches for the stem, leaves and flower.
4. Stitch the buttonhole stitch for the outer edge of the flower.
5. Stitch the yellow chain stitch of the flower.

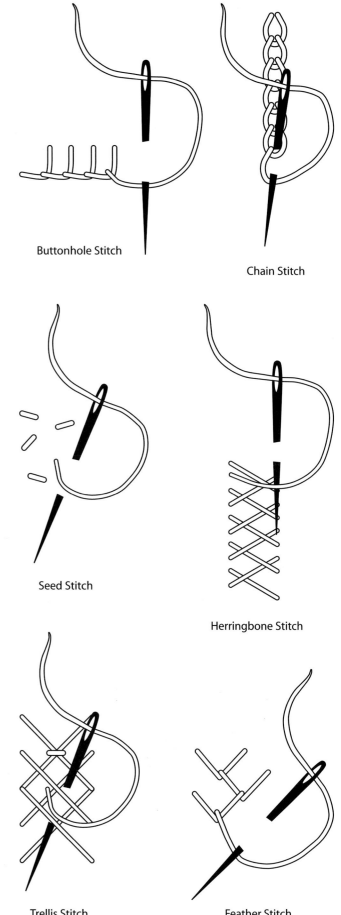

Buttonhole Stitch

Chain Stitch

Seed Stitch

Herringbone Stitch

Trellis Stitch

Feather Stitch

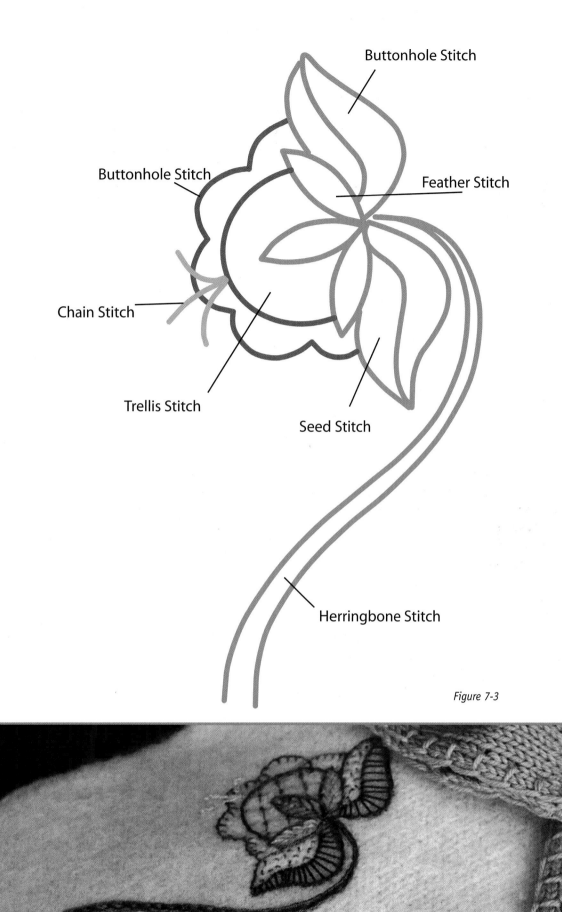

Buttonhole Stitch

Buttonhole Stitch

Feather Stitch

Chain Stitch

Trellis Stitch

Seed Stitch

Herringbone Stitch

Figure 7-3

Top-Down Cape or Poncho with Duplicate Stitch Embroidery

EASY

BULKY
5
BULKY
Abultado

A great advantage to beginning a poncho or cape at the neckline is that you can knit until your outfit is just the right size for you, trying it on as you go to see if it has reached the length you want. If you are short on yarn—or time—this is a wonderful way to work, since you can quickly make a capelet or short poncho instead of the full-length one shown. Another advantage is that you can add details at the edge by working a row or two of a different yarn to finish off your creation.

Finished Size
34" circumference neck opening
28" from neckline to center front or back point
19" from neckline to arm edge
Gauge
7 sts and 11 rows = 4"

MATERIALS

· 3 balls (142yd/129m) bulky-weight novelty yarn*
· 1 ball (77yd/70m) medium-weight novelty yarn*
· Size 17 (12.75mm) needles
· Stitch markers
· Tapestry needle for embroidery
· Clasp, needle and thread (for cape option)

*Used in this project: 3 balls Patons' Divine (79.5% acrylic/18% mohair/2.5% polyester, 142yd/129m, 3.5oz/100g), color #06117 Denim Storm, and 1 ball Patons' Cha Cha (100% nylon, 77yd/70m, 1.75oz/50g), color #02015 Night Club.

PONCHO INSTRUCTIONS

Note: All inc sts are made by k into the front and the back of the next st.
CO 60 sts and join into a circle.
Row 1: K28, inc 1, pm, inc 1, k 28, inc 1, pm, inc 1 - 64 sts.
Row 2: K.
Row 3: P.
Row 4: K to 1 st before marker, inc 1 in st before marker and inc 1 in st after marker, k to 1 st before next marker, inc 1 in st before marker and inc 1 in st after marker - 68 sts.
Row 5: K.
Rep (rows 4 and 5) 25 times or until poncho is the desired length.
BO and weave in ends.

CAPE INSTRUCTIONS

CO 60 sts.
Row 1: Inc 1, k 28 sts, inc 1, pm, inc 1, k 28 sts, inc 1 - 64 sts.
Row 2: K.
Row 3 and all RS rows: Inc 1, k to st before marker, inc 1 in st before and inc 1 in st after marker, k to last st, inc 1 - 68 sts.
Row 4 and all WS rows: P.
Rep (rows 3 and 4) 25 times or until cape is the desired length.
Sew each side of the clasp to the top corners of the neckline opening of the cape.

DUPLICATE STITCH EMBROIDERY

Embroidering in duplicate stitch is an easy technique in which you duplicate the path of the knit stitch, working in a different color than the knitting. Here's how for the black zigzag pattern on the cape or poncho:

1. Thread the tapestry needle with a 24" length of the black eyelash yarn.

2. Insert the needle through the finished knitting from back to front at the base of the sixth stitch down and one stitch to the right of the center back of the poncho or cape, leaving a 4" to 6" tail to weave in behind the embroidery later.

3. Following the path of the knitted stitch you are covering, pass behind the stitch in the row above and then back through the point where you first inserted the needle. You will have made one V-shaped stitch that covers one knit stitch in the poncho or cape.

4. Repeat steps 2 and 3, making your next "V" one stitch to the right and one row up from the first stitch. Continue in a slanting upward line until you have five stitches.

5. Change direction, making your stitches one stitch to the right and one row down each time, until you have five more stitches in that direction.

6. Change direction after each five stitches so you create a zigzag pattern below the neckline all the way to the center front.

7. Work the same pattern on the other side of the cape or poncho, beginning to the left of the center back and working towards the left.

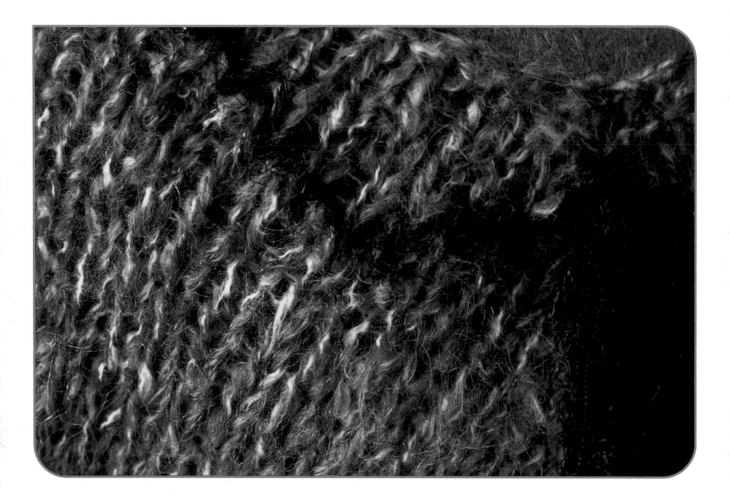

Fringes and Edgings

There are so many treatments you can add to the bottom of a scarf to make it special. The following are just a few possibilities to get your thoughts going on others. Most of these scarves are just basic, long rectangles with details added at the ends, though some have more designs throughout.

Fuchsia Gathered-End Scarf

This scarf and the one that follows it are not really traditional ties, but they can be tied like a man's tie and worn like one. In the model shown here, the scarf is tied loosely in the traditional manner to give it a more feminine appeal.

BEGINNER

SUPER FINE
1
SUPER FIN
Super Fino

Finished Size 2" x 56"
Gauge
(Measure in stockinette stitch.)
16 sts and 18 rows = 4"

MATERIALS
- 1 ball (198yd/180m) fingering-weight yarn*
- Size 9 (5.5mm) needles
- Tapestry needle

*Used in this project: 1 ball S. Charles Callezione's Ritratto (28% mohair, 53% rayon, 10% nylon, 9% polyester, 198yd/180m, 1.75oz/50g), color #77 Fuchsia.

INSTRUCTIONS
CO 30 sts, leaving a 10" tail.
Work in St st until there is about 10" yarn left.
Thread the yarn into a tapestry needle and pass through the rem sts twice, gathering them tightly tog.
Weave in end.
Thread the beg 10" tail into tapestry needle and pass through the beg sts twice, gathering them tightly tog.
Weave in end.

Silver Knotted Tie

SUPER FINE
1
SUPER FIN
Super Fino

This tie is similar to the Fuchsia Gathered-End Scarf on pages 98 and 99, but takes on a completely different look just by knotting off the ends instead of letting them hang as-is. It is more like a bolo with the abalone ring holding it in place.

Finished Size 1" x 38"
Gauge
(Measure in stockinette stitch.)
20 sts and 18 rows = 4"

MATERIALS
- 1 cone (108yd/100m) fingering weight metallic yarn*
- Size 8 (5mm) needles

*Used in this project: 1 cone Lincatex's Gold Rush (80% rayon, 20% metallised polyester, 108yd/100m, .9oz/25g), color #5 Silver.

INSTRUCTIONS
CO 20 sts, leaving a 10" tail.
Work in St st until there is about 10" yarn left.
Thread the yarn into a tapestry needle and pass
 through the rem sts twice, gathering them tightly
 tog.
Weave in end.
Thread the beg 10" tail into tapestry needle and pass
 through the beg sts twice, gathering them tightly
 tog.
Weave in end.
Tie ends of the scarf in overhand knot, as in
 Figure 8-1 below.

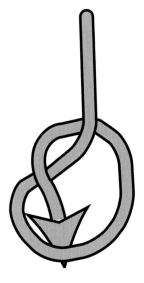

Figure 8-1

Knotted Burgundy Sparkles

EASY

This fluid yarn has just the right touch of sparkle to make this easy wrap perfect for an elegant evening out on the town. For added glitz, you can make the knotted fringe longer with more knots than shown, or simpler with just one or two rows of knots. It's up to you.

Finished Size
18" x 72", not including 9" fringe
Gauge
(Measure in stockinette stitch.)
20 sts and 29 rows = 4"

MATERIALS

· 8 balls (166yd/151m) sport-weight metallic yarn*
· Size 6 (4.25mm) needle
· Size G crochet hook

*Used in this project: 8 balls Patons' Brilliant (69% acrylic, 31% polyester, 166yd/151m, 1.75oz/50g), color #4430 Beautiful Burgundy.

INSTRUCTIONS

CO 90 sts.
Work in St st until 72" from beg.
BO and weave in ends.

FRINGE

1. Cut 60 25" lengths of yarn.

2. Fold each 25" strand in half.

3. Use crochet hook to attach folded strands to the ends of the scarf, spacing them three stitches apart.

4. Hold the first two groups of fringe together as one and make an overhand knot about 1" from the scarf, as in Figure 8-2.

Figure 8-2

5. Repeat step 4 for each pair of fringe groups across the scarf. This is the first row of knots.

6. Separate the knotted groups of four into pairs.

7. Skip the first pair and hold the second pair and third pair together as one and make an overhand knot about 1" from the first row of knots, as in Figure 8-3.

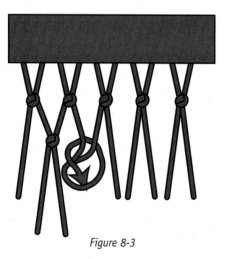

Figure 8-3

8. Repeat step 7 across the scarf. There will be one pair of fringe strands left at the end. This is the second row of knots.

9. Begin with the first pair of strands that was skipped in the second row and make knots of four strands again about 1" from the second row of knots, as in Figure 8-4.

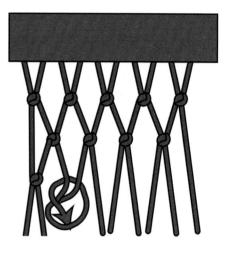

Figure 8-4

10. Repeat step 9 all the way across the scarf for the third and final row of knots.

PONCHO VARIATION

You will need about the same amount of yarn as for the wrap.

CO 80 sts.

Work in St st until 33" from beg.

BO and weave in ends.

Rep instructions to make another rectangle.

Sew the rectangles tog as in the Easy Evening Poncho on page 53.

Make a shorter version of the knotted fringe all around the edges by cutting the fringe in 18" lengths instead of 25" lengths and making the knots closer together.

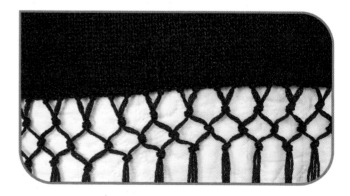

Tassel Scarf

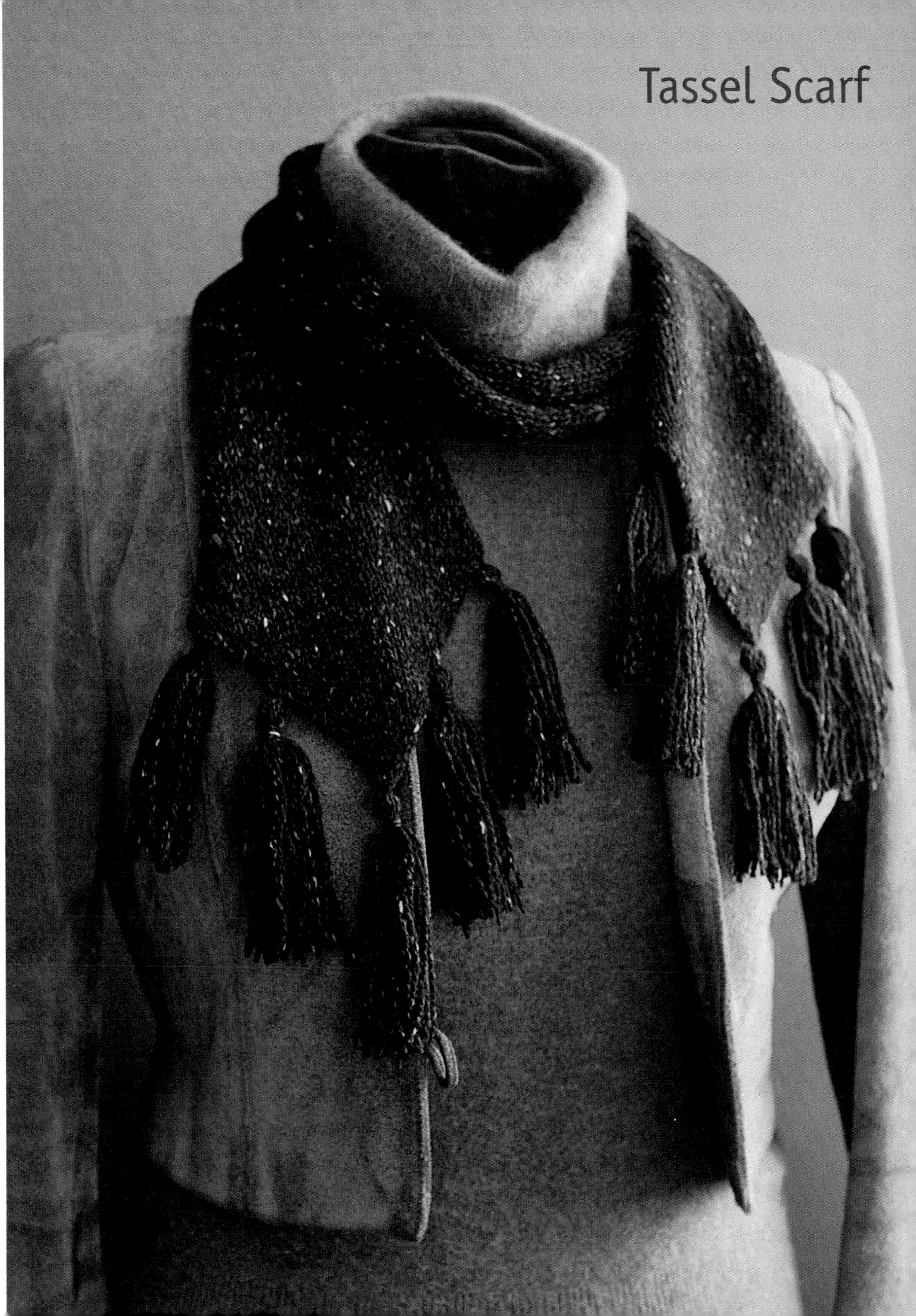

Tassel Scarf

EASY

Tassels are a great little item to make for anything from a hat to a scarf to a shawl. Long and delicate, or short and fat, there is a lot you can do with a tassel to make it a little different to add to your design. These basic mid-sized tassels are loosely spaced on the pointed ends of this rich, purple tweed yarn, giving it weight at the ends and a little pizzazz.

Finished Size
6½" x 52", not including 4½" tassels
Gauge
(Measure in stockinette stitch.)
20 sts and 28 rows = 4"

MATERIALS

· 2 balls (191yd/175m) sport-weight yarn*
· Size 7 (4.5mm) needle
· 3" x 5" piece cardboard
· Tapestry needle

*Used in this project: 2 balls Rowan's Felted Tweed (50% merino wool/ 25% alpaca/25% rayon, 191yd/175m, 1.75oz/50g), color #151.

INSTRUCTIONS

Work in St st throughout.
CO 1 st.
Inc 1 st at beg of each row until there are 32 sts.
Work 5 rows even.
On the next RS row, k1, dec 1, yo, k26, yo, dec 1, k1.
Rep this 6-row patt 50 more times.
Work 5 rows even.
Dec 1 st at beg of each row until 2 sts rem.
Cut yarn and pass through rem sts.
Weave in end.

TASSELS

1. Wrap the yarn around the 3" x 5" cardboard 16 times, as in Figure 8-5, sliding a 12" piece of yarn under the wraps, pulling it tight, and tying it into a square knot.

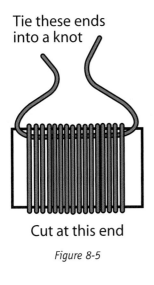

Tie these ends
into a knot

Cut at this end

Figure 8-5

2. Slide the wrapped yarn off the cardboard and cut the wraps at the opposite end of the knot.

3. Thread an 18" piece of yarn and wrap it tightly around the folded end of the tassel about ½" from the knotted end, wrapping toward the knotted end.

4. Pass back through the wrapping, as in Figure 8-6, and pull both ends tight to secure the wrap.

Figure 8-6

5. Knot the end closest to the folded yarn and pass it back down toward the cut ends of the tassel.

6. Use the tails of the yarn originally tied into a square knot to attach the tassels to the scarf.

7. Repeat steps 1 through 6 nine more times.

Purple Suede-Fringed Poncho

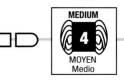

EASY

MEDIUM
4
MOYEN
Medio

This poncho begins with just one stitch and is increased after row 5 at the sides by making yarn-overs near each end on every other row. The yarn-overs come in handy when you add the fringe edging since you attach the fringe into eyelets created by the yarn-overs. This ensures that the spacing of the fringe is perfectly even along the edges. The neck opening is finished by adding fringe directly to groups of stitches still on the needle so you have very little binding off in this project.

Finished Size
30" circumference neck opening
24" from neckline to center front or back point
13" from neckline to arm edge
Gauge
17 sts and 23 rows = 4"

MATERIALS
· 7 balls (120yd/111m) medium-weight yarn*
· Size 8 (5mm) needles
· Size I crochet hook
· Stitch holder

*Used in this project: 7 balls Berroco's Suede (100% nylon, 120yd/111m, 1.75oz/50g), color #3745 Purple.

INSTRUCTIONS
Poncho body (make two):
CO 1 st.
Row 1: K into front and back of st - 2 sts.
Row 2 and all WS rows: P.
Row 3: (K into front and back of st) rep twice - 4 sts.
Row 5: K2, yo, k2 - 5 sts.
Row 7: K2, yo, k1, yo, k2 - 7 sts.
Row 9: K2, yo, k to the last 2 sts, yo, k2 - 9 sts.
Rep (rows 8 and 9) 60 times.

Neck opening:
Place the center 41 sts on st holder.
Work each shoulder side separately by cont the yo inc along the outside edges and work even on the neck edge, working 6 more rows.
BO the shoulder edges and weave in ends.
Sew the front and back shoulder seams together.

Neckline:
Beg at the neck edge of the shoulder seam, with new length of yarn and working from the RS, pick up and k 4 sts along one side of the neck along the last 6 rows of the shoulder (A), all 41 sts from the st holder (B), 4 sts from the other side of the neck along the last 6 rows of the shoulder (C), 4 sts from the next piece along the last 6 rows of the shoulder (D), the 41 sts from the other st holder (E), and 4 sts from the last side of the neck along the last 6 rows of the shoulder (F), as shown in Figure 8-7 above right.
Working in the rnd, k 3 rows.
Do not BO.

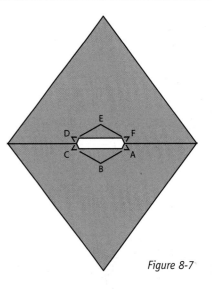

Figure 8-7

NECKLINE FRINGE
1. Cut 78 7½"-long strips of yarn in groups of three (26 groups).
2. Use the crochet hook to pick up the next four stitches off the knitting needle.
3. Fold one of the three-strand groups of 7½"-long strands in half and pull it through the four stitches on the crochet hook.
4. Pull the ends of the group of strands through the loop on the hook, creating a small tassel.
5. Repeat steps 2 through 4 for the rest of the stitches around the neckline. (You may have to pick up only three stitches on the last few groups of stitches.)

FRINGE
1. Cut 198 7½"-long strips of yarn in groups of three (66 groups).
2. Use the crochet hook to attach each three-strand group into every other yarn-over hole along the sides of the poncho. Add one more at each point.

Fringed Wrap

This luscious wrap is so comfortable and so fun to wear and it's all because of the unending path of fringe surrounding all the edges. Both the knitting and the fringing are easy to do, though it takes a lot of time to add all those little strips of yarn to every inch of the perimeter of the piece!

EASY

Finished Size
20" x 70", not including 4½" fringe
Gauge
(Measure in stockinette stitch.)
15 sts and 20 rows = 4"

MATERIALS

- 14 balls (81yd/75m) heavy worsted-weight yarn*
- Size 9 (5.5mm) needles
- 3" x 5" piece cardboard
- Size H (5mm) crochet hook

*Used in this project: 14 balls Tahki Stacy Charles, Inc.'s Bunny (50% merino wool/25% alpaca/25% acrylic, 81yd/75m, 1.75oz/50g), color #018.

INSTRUCTIONS

CO 75 sts.
Work in St st until 70" from beg.
BO and weave in ends.

FRINGE

1. Wrap yarn around the 3" x 5" piece of cardboard and cut at one end, creating 320 10" lengths. (You will need to do this in groups of about 15 wraps, not all 320 at once.)

2. Use the crochet hook to attach each strand to the edge of the wrap, as in Figure 8-8, one for each stitch along the 20" sides and one every other row for the 70" sides. Add an extra one or two at each corner.

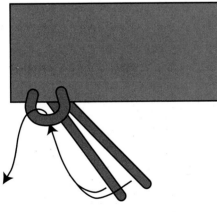

Figure 8-8

3. Cut more 10" strips if needed.

PONCHO VARIATION

You will need about the same amount of yarn as used for the wrap.
CO 60 sts.
Work in St st until 34" from beg.
BO and weave in ends.
Rep instructions to make another rectangle.
Sew the rectangles tog as in the Easy Evening Poncho on page 53.
Fringe around the edges and neckline as for the wrap.

Striped Snake I-Cord Scarf

EASY

MEDIUM
4
MOYEN
Medio

Fun, fun, fun. This little snake coils around itself, so why not coil it around your neck to keep you toasty warm on a cold day? Hand-dyed variegated yarn is always fun to play with. To create the sweeping color pattern in the I-cord fringe, be careful to cut the same short length (about 3") of the beginning and ending tail of yarn while making the I-cord, and working each piece in succession from the same ball of yarn.

Finished Size
2" x 72", not including 4½" fringe
Gauge
(Measure in garter stitch.)
18 sts and 24 rows = 4"

MATERIALS
· 1 skein (500yd/462m) worsted-weight variegated yarn with color changes at regular intervals*
· Size 8 (5mm) double-pointed needles

*Used in this project: 1 skein Lorna's Laces' Fisherman (100% wool, 500yd/462m), color Shadow.

INSTRUCTIONS
CO 3 sts, leaving a 1½" tail.
Make a 26-row I-cord, encasing the tail as you work.
Cut the working thread to about 3" (just enough to weave in later).
Slide the finished I-cord onto a spare dpn.

Rep until there are 24 I-cord lengths, 12 on each of 2 dpn.
Take 1 of the dpn of I-cord and work across, k2 sts, then k the next 2 sts tog, rep across - 27 sts.
Work several rows St st, then weave in the ends of I-cord.
Cont St st until 72" from beg or desired length less about 5", including the fringe.
Beg the other end of the scarf in the same way, making 27 sts across and k for about 1".
Graft the 2 pieces tog.
Weave in ends.

Draping Loops I-Cord Scarf

INTERMEDIATE

LIGHT
3
LEGER
Ligero

I-cord has a ton of possibilities for design. This simple pattern drapes well and can be worn in more than one way, each having its own special look. The trick with this kind of I-cord layout is to arrange the I-cord the way you want it, passing a double-pointed needle through the cord at the points where you want it to end, cutting the cord about ½" to 1" beyond that point and then unraveling the cord and passing the needle through the live stitches where you want the cord to end.

Finished Size
9" x 66", not including 4½" draping fringe
Gauge
(Measure in stockinette stitch.)
20 sts and 24 rows = 4"

MATERIALS

· 4 balls (137yd/125m) brown DK weight yarn*
· Size 7 (4.5mm) needles
· Size 7 (4.5mm) double-pointed needles

*Used in this project: 4 balls Jaeger's Extra Fine Merino Double Knitting (100% extra fine merino wool, 137yd/125m, 1.75oz/50g), color #975 Tweed.

Pierce through I-cord

Cut and unravel

Repeat for each loop

Figure 8-9

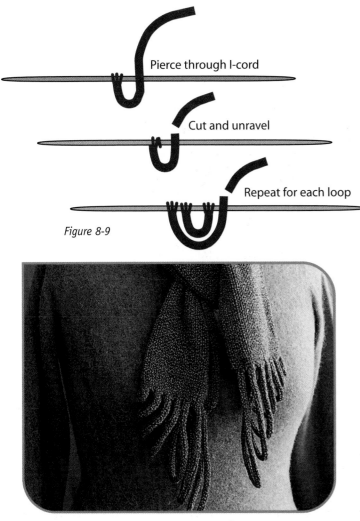

An entirely different look is accomplished when the I-cord loops are not laying flat.

INSTRUCTIONS

Use dpn to make a 3-st I-cord that is about 70" long.

Cut the working yarn 3" from the knitting, and loop the I-cord around so you can slide it onto the dpn, creating the size of the first center loop.

Cut through the I-cord about ½" from the dpn and unravel the stitches until you reach the dpn, as shown in Figure 8-9.

Slide that end off the dpn and then slide it back on so you pick up each of the 3 sts.

Unravel the cut end of the remaining I-cord so you have enough yarn to weave in later (about 3") and slide it onto the dpn next to the first loop, being careful to pick up each of the 3 sts.

Wrap the I-cord around the first loop so it hangs about ½" lower than that first loop.

Pass the dpn through the I-cord to hold it in place.

Cut through the I-cord about ½" away from the dpn, unravel and then reposition the end, picking up the 3 sts the same way you worked the first loop.

Rep for each loop, until there are 7 loops.

Change to the single-pointed needles, attach a new strand of yarn and k across all the I-cord stitches - 42 sts.

P back.

Working in St st, add 4 sts at the beg of the next two rows - 46, then 50 sts.

Work in St st until 33" from beg, not including I-cord fringe.

Rep the whole process for the other end of the scarf.

Graft the 2 pieces tog.

Fold the 4 st selvages to the inside along the sides of the scarf and sew in place. Steam press.

Celtic Braid I-Cord Scarf

I don't know if this really is a Celtic braid, but it's fun to make and wear and it looks a little Celtic to me. The I-cord is worked similar to the Draping Loops Scarf in that you will need to cut and unravel the I-cord at the top of the braid to prepare for knitting the scarf.

Finished Size
9" x 36", not including 12" braided fringe
Gauge
(Measure in garter stitch.)
17 sts and 23 rows = 4"

MATERIALS

· 3 balls (218yd/200m) camel-colored worsted-weight yarn*
· Size 9 (5.5mm) needles
· Size 9 (5.5mm) double-pointed needles
· Stitch holder

*Used in this project: 3 balls Knit One Crochet Too's Parfait Solids
(100% pure wool, 218yd/200m, 3.5oz/100g), color #1893.

INSTRUCTIONS

Making the braided I-cord fringe:
Use the dpn to make 4 35"-long 4-st I-cords, leaving
  each with a 3" tail.
Unravel the beg of the I-cords so there is enough yarn
  to weave in later.
Use the standard needle to pick up the sts of each
  end of 1 cord.
Rep for the other 3 cords, creating 4 looped I-cords.
Braid the pairs of cord as shown in Figure 8-10
  and Figure 8-11.
Tack the bottom of the braiding about 4" from the
  ends.

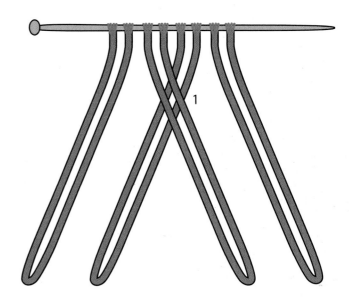

Figure 8-10

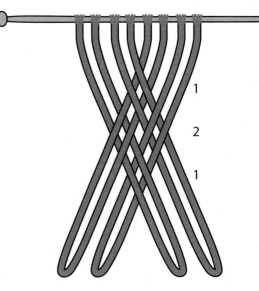

Figure 8-11

Knitting the scarf:

Row 1: Attach a new length of yarn and k across the I-cords - 32 sts.

Row 2: P.

Row 3: Inc, k to the last st, inc - 34 sts.

Row 4: K1, p to last st, k1.

Row 5: Inc, k to the last st, inc - 36 sts.

Row 6: K2, p to last 2 sts, k2.

Row 7: Inc, k to the last st, inc - 38 sts.

Row 8: K3, p to last 3 sts, k3.

Row 9: Inc, k to the last st, inc - 40 sts.

Row 10: K4, p to last 4 sts, k4.

Row 11: K.

Rep rows 10 and 11 until 18" from beg, not including fringe.

Move to stitch holder. Set aside.

Rep the process of making the braided I-cord fringe and knitting the scarf for a second piece.

Graft the 2 pieces tog.

Weave in ends.

Elegant Chenille Bead-Fringed Scarf

Elegant Chenille Bead-Fringed Scarf

Yarn with a sheen like this and a fabulous silky feel just cries out for beads to complement its texture. Here the scarf is just a basic stockinette stitch rectangle, but when you add a simple two-level fringe in pearl and dichroic glass beads, you have created a Rolls Royce of scarves—simple, elegant and lush!

 **INTERMEDIATE**

BULKY
5
BULKY
Abultado

Finished Size
6" x 47", not including 2¼" beaded fringe
Gauge
(Measure in stockinette stitch.)
11 sts and 13 rows = 4"

MATERIALS
- 2 balls (38yd/35m) bulky weight chenille yarn*
- Size 11 (8mm) needles
- 76 size 5 dichroic beads
- 38 ⅜"-long faceted drop beads
- 114 accent pearl beads
- 38 ⅛" faceted beads
- 152 spacer beads
- Less than 4 grams size 11 seed beads
- 7 grams size 8 seed beads
- Size 11 beading needle
- Beading thread to match

*Used in this project: 2 balls Plymouth Yarn's Sinsation (80% rayon/20% wool, 38yd/35m, 1.75oz/50g), color #3321 Mint.

INSTRUCTIONS
CO 20 sts.
Work in St st until 47" from beg.
BO and weave in ends.

FRINGE
1. Attach a 24" length of beading thread to the corner of the scarf.
2. String the shorter bead pattern, as in Figure 8-12, skipping the last three beads strung and passing back through the rest of the beads.

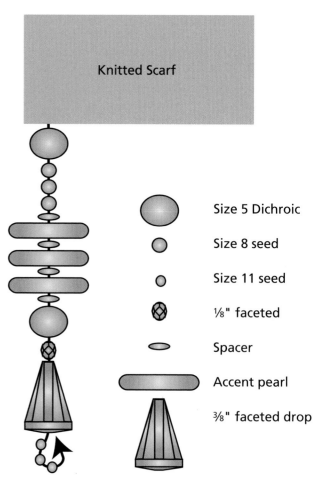

Knitted Scarf

⬤	Size 5 Dichroic
○	Size 8 seed
○	Size 11 seed
⬡	⅛" faceted
⬭	Spacer
▭	Accent pearl
▽	⅜" faceted drop

Figure 8-12

3. Make a small knot in the yarn to anchor the thread in place.

4. Pass the needle to the next stitch along the bottom edge of the scarf and string the longer bead pattern, as in Figure 8-13, in the same manner as the shorter string.

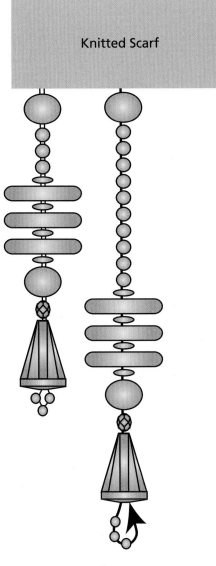

Figure 8-13

Tapered Ruffles Scarf

Frilly, feminine and easy-to-knit are adjectives that come together in this tapered-end ruffled scarf. The ruffle is just knit in stockinette stitch until the desired length and then decreased across two right-side rows. You work short rows to taper the scarf without any special treatment, just knitting part way across and then turning back and working in the other direction. By not slipping a stitch, you create a small eyelet that adds to the design. The luxurious mohair blend yarn is twined with a thin bumpy textured synthetic, creating an interesting texture and color change throughout the piece.

INTERMEDIATE

FINE **2** FIN Fino

Finished Size
4½" x 62"
Gauge
22 sts and 19 rows = 4"

MATERIALS
· 2 skeins (125yd/114m) sport-weight yarn*
· Size 8 (5mm) needle

*Used in this project: 2 skeins Knit One Crochet Too's Melange (48% viscose/36% mohair/16% nylon, 125yd/114m, 1.75oz/50g), color #0803.

INSTRUCTIONS
CO 100 sts.
Work in St st for 20 rows (about 2½").
On the next RS row, k2tog, rep across - 50 sts.
P the next row.
On the next row, k2tog, rep across - 25 sts.
K the next row.
Work short rows for point, as follows:

- Row 1: K1, turn.
- Row 2: P1, turn.
- Row 3: K2, turn.
- Row 4: P2, turn.
- Row 5: K3, turn.
- Row 6: P3, turn.
- Row 7: K4, turn.
- Row 8: P4, turn
- Row 9: K5, turn.
- Row 10: P5, turn.

Cont k 1 more st in each row and then p back to the end on the following row until you are working across all 25 sts.

Work in St st until 44" from the end of the ruffle or desired length, less the other ruffle.
Work short rows for point, as follows:

- Row 1: K24, turn.
- Row 2: P24, turn.
- Row 3: K23, turn.
- Row 4: P23, turn.
- Row 5: K22, turn.
- Row 6: P22, turn.
- Row 7: K21, turn.
- Row 8: P21, turn
- Row 9: K20, turn.
- Row 10: P20, turn.

Cont k 1 less st in each row and then p the same number of sts as the previous row until you k1 st and p1 st.
Inc for ruffle, as follows:

- On the next row, k into the front and back of each st across - 50 sts.
- P next row.
- On the next row, k into the front and back of ea st across - 100 sts.
- Work even in St st until ruffle is the same length as the beginning ruffle.

BO and weave in ends.
Block.

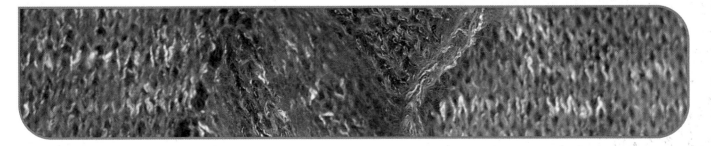

Delicate Eyelet Bead-Fringed Scarf

This taper-ended, delicate peachy-salmon scarf sprinkled with eyelets is perfectly topped off with an easy, light-beaded fringe. And anchoring each dangle at an eyelet along the edge makes it easy work to bead.

Finished Size
4½" x 43", not including 2" beaded fringe

Gauge
(Measure in stockinette stitch.)
22 sts and 28 rows = 4"

INTERMEDIATE

FINE
2
FIN
Fino

MATERIALS

- 2 balls (218yd/200m) sport-weight yarn*
- Size 4 (3.5mm) needles
- Stitch holder
- 7 grams size 11 cream-colored seed beads
- 46 ¼" pearl beads
- 46 size 5 triangle beads
- 92 size 8 triangle beads
- Size 11 beading needle
- Beading thread to match

*Used in this project: 2 skeins Jaeger's Trinity (40% silk/35% cotton/25% polyamide, 218yd/200m, 1.75oz/50g), color #434 Pale Peach.

INSTRUCTIONS

CO 3 sts.
Follow Figure 8-14 or the line-by-line instructions below, working row 1 through row 46 and then repeating row 27 through row 46 six more times.
Row 1 and all odd-numbered rows: P.
Row 2: (K1, yo) twice, k1 - 5 sts.
Row 4: K1, yo, k3, yo, k1 - 7 sts.
Row 6: K1, yo, k5, yo, k1 - 9 sts.
Row 8: K1, yo, k1, (k2tog, yo) twice, k2, yo, k1 - 11 sts.
Row 10: K1, yo, k3, k2tog, yo, k4, yo, k1 - 13 sts.
Row 12: K1, yo, k11, yo, k1 - 15 sts.
Row 14: K1, yo, k13, yo, k1 - 17 sts.
Row 16: K1, yo, k15, yo, k1 - 19 sts.
Row 18: K1, yo, k2, (k2tog, yo) twice, k4, (k2tog, yo) twice, k3, yo, k1 - 21 sts.
Row 20: K1, yo, k4, k2tog, yo, k6, k2tog, yo, k5, yo, k1 - 23 sts.
Row 22: K1, yo, k21, yo, k1 - 25 sts.
Row 24: K.
Row 26: K.

Row 28: K2, ((k2tog, yo) twice, k4) twice, (k2tog, yo) twice, k3.
Row 30: K3, (k2tog, yo, k6) twice, k2tog, yo, k4.
Row 32: K.
Row 34: K.
Row 36: K6, (k2tog, yo, k4) twice, k3.
Row 38: K7, (k2tog, yo, k6) twice, k2.
Row 44: K.
Row 46: K.
Move to holder.
Rep the instructions to make the other end of the scarf.
Work row 27 through 31.
Graft the 2 pieces tog.
Weave in ends.

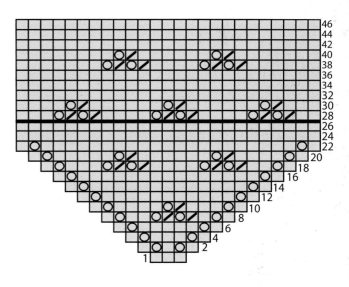

☐ knit on right side, purl on wrong side
◩ k2tog
◪ yo

Figure 8-14

FRINGE

1. Attach a 24" length of thread to one of the upper corner eyelets along the end of the scarf.

2. String the pattern of beads, as in Figure 8-15, skipping the last three beads strung and passing the needle back up through the rest of the beads.

3. Tie a small knot on the scarf and pass through the next eyelet.

4. Repeat steps 2 and 3 for each of the eyelets along the edge of the scarf, as well as the center bottom point.

5. Weave in ends.

Knitted Scarf

20 size 11 seed beads

Size 5 Triangle

4mm pearl

Size 8 seed

Size 11 seed

⅛" faceted

¼" bugle

Figure 8-15

Supply Sources

Always check with your local knitting, yarn or craft stores for knitting supplies, tools, embellishments and books.

YARN COMPANIES

Baabajoes Wool Company
P.O. Box 260604
Lakewood, CO 80226
www.baabajoeswool.com

Bernat, Patons and Lily Yarns
P.O. Box 40
Listowel, Ontario, Canada N4W 3H3
www.bernat.com
www.patonsyarns.com
www.lilyyarns.com

Berroco, Inc.
P.O. Box 367
14 Elmdale Road
Uxbridge, MA 01569
www.berroco.com

Brown Sheep Co., Inc.
100662 County Road 16
Mitchell, NE 69357
www.brownsheep.com

Blue Sky Alpacas, Inc.
P.O. Box 387
St. Francis, MN 55070
www.blueskyalpacas.com

Cascade Yarns
1224 Andover Park E
Tukwila, WA 98188
(800) 548-1048
www.cascadeyarns.com

Classic Elite Yarns
122 Western Ave.
Lowell, MA 01851

Crystal Palace Yarns
160 23rd St.
Richmond, CA 94804
(510) 237-9988
www.straw.com

Dale of Norway
N16 W23390 Stoneridge Drive #A
Waukesha, WI 53188
(262) 544-1996
www.dale.no

Harrisville Designs
P.O. Box 806
Harrisville, NH 03450
(603) 827-3333
www.harrisville.com

Ironstone Yarns
P.O. Box 8
Las Vegas, NM 87701

JCA, Artful Yarns, Reynolds
35 Scales Lane
Townsend, MA 01469-1094

Knit One Crochet Too
91 Tandberg Trail
Windham, ME 04062
(207) 892-9625
www.knitonecrochettoo.com

Lion Brand
34 W. 15th St.
New York, NY 10011
(800) 258-9276
www.lionbrand.com

Lorna's Laces Yarns
4229 N. Honore St.
Chicago, IL 60613
(773) 935-3803
www.lornaslaces.net

Plymouth Yarn
P.O. Box 28
Bristol, PA 19007
(215) 788-0459
www.plymouthyarn.com

Rowan, Jaeger
Westminster Fibers
4 Townsend W Unit 8
Nashua, NH 03063

**Tahki-StacyCharles
and Filatura Di Crosa**
70-30 80th St., Building 36
Ridgewood, NY 11384
(800) 338-yarn
www.tahkistacycharles.com

Trendsetter Yarns
16745 Saticoy St., #101
Van Nuys, CA 91406
www.trendsetteryarns.com

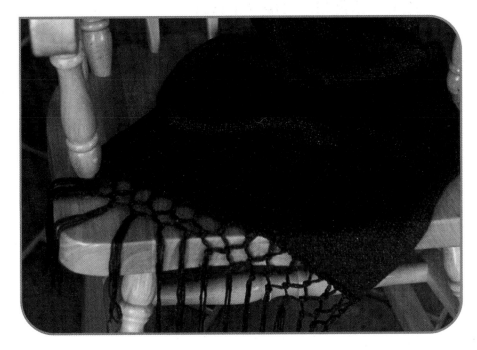

EMBELLISHMENTS

Bead Heaven
A division of Halcraft USA, Inc.
New York, NY 10010
www.halcraft.com

Blue Moon Beads
7855 Hayvenhurst Ave.
Van Nuys, CA 91406
www.bluemoonbeads.com

The Caron Collection
55 Old South Ave.
Stratford, CT 06615-7315
www.caron-net.com

Cousin Corporation
P.O. Box 2939
Largo, FL 33779
(800) 366-2687
www.cousin.com

Creative Castle
2321 Michael Drive
Newbury Park, CA 91320-3233
(805) 499-1377
www.creativecastle.com

Darice
13000 Darice Parkway, Park 82
Strongsville, OH 44149
(866) 432-7423
www.darice.com

Fire Mountain Gems and Beads
1 Fire Mountain Way
Grants Pass, OR 97526-2373
(800) 423-2319
www.firemountaingems.com

Rings & Things
P.O. Box 450
214 N. Wall St., Suite 990
Spokane, WA 99210-0450
(509) 624-8565
www.rings-things.com

Westrim Crafts
7855 Hayvenhurst Ave.
Van Nyes, CA 91406
(800) 727-2727
www.westrimcrafts.com

KNITTING TOOLS

Addi Turbo Needles
P.O. Box 88110
Seattle, WA 98138-2110
www.scacelknitting.com

Boye Needle
A product of Wrights
85 South St.
West Warren, MA 01092
www.wrights.com

Brittany Hooks and Needles
(707) 877-1881
www.brittanyneedles.com

Clover Needlecraft, Inc.
13438 Alondra Blvd.
Cerrilos, CA 90703
www.clover-usa.com

Crystal Palace Yarns
160 23rd St.
Richmond, CA 94804
www.straw.com

Susan Bates
A product of Coats & Clark
P.O. Box 12229
Greenville, SC 29612
(800) 648-1479
www.coatsandclark.com

OTHER RESOURCES

Craft Yarn Council of America (CYCA)
P.O. Box 9
Gastonia, NC 28053
(704) 824-7838
www.craftyarncouncil.com

KP Books
700 E. State St.
Iola, WI 54990-0001
(888) 457-2873
www.krause.com

The Knitting Guild Association (TKGA)
P.O. Box 3388
Zanesville, OH 43702-3388
(740) 452-4541
www.tkga.com

The National NeedleArts Association (TNNA)
P.O. Box 3388
1100-H Brandywine Blvd.
Zanesville, OH 43702-3388
(740) 455-6773
www.tnna.org